THE ATTACK ON AMERICA: SEPTEMBER 11, 2001

Other books in the At Issue series:

THE ATTACK ON AMERICA: SEPTEMBER 11, 2001

William Dudley, *Book Editor*

Daniel Leone, *President*
Bonnie Szumski, *Publisher*
Scott Barbour, *Managing Editor*

GREENHAVEN PRESS
SAN DIEGO, CALIFORNIA

GALE GROUP
™
THOMSON LEARNING
Detroit • New York • San Diego • San Francisco
Boston • New Haven, Conn. • Waterville, Maine
London • Munich

Library of Congress Cataloging-in-Publication Data

The attack on America: September 11, 2001 / William Dudley, book editor.
        p. cm. — (At issue) (An opposing viewpoints series)
    Includes bibliographical references and index.
    ISBN 0-7377-1292-9 (lib. bdg. : alk. paper) —
ISBN 0-7377-1293-7 (pbk. : alk. paper)
    1. info. I. Dudley, William, 1964–   . II. Series: At issue (San Diego, Calif.) III. Series: Opposing viewpoints series (Unnumbered)

    x   2002
—dc21   2001
                                                                          CIP

Copyright © 2002 by Greenhaven Press,
an imprint of The Gale Group
10911 Technology Place, San Diego, CA 92127

Printed in the U.S.A.

Contents

Introduction

On September 11, 2001, four passenger planes were hijacked by terrorists. Two of the planes were flown into the twin towers of the World Trade Center (WTC) in New York City, causing huge fires that led to the collapse of the towers less than two hours later. One plane crashed into the Pentagon building in Washington, D.C. The last plane crashed in a field in Pennsylvania; it is believed the hijackers had planned to also crash this plane into a building or landmark, but were foiled by the actions of the plane's passengers. Many of these horrific events, including the second plane's crash into the World Trade Center and the collapse of the towers, were witnessed live by millions of television viewers. It was by far the worst terrorist attack on American soil; conservative columnist George F. Will labeled it "the most lethal terrorism in human experience."

As the dust settled in New York and Washington, Americans were left to ponder what the attacks meant for the nation. In search of a historical precedent or point of comparison, many Americans reached back to Japan's surprise assault on Pearl Harbor on December 7, 1941, another "day of infamy" in which the United States was suddenly attacked. In both instances, a seemingly secure nation was jolted by massive assaults on its own soil. "As Pearl Harbor snapped America out of a false sense of security," NBC news anchor and author Tom Brokaw writes, "September 11 had a similar effect on young Americans."

The comparisons Brokaw and others made between the two dates dealt not only with the attacks themselves, but also how the American people responded to them. Many people wondered whether the resolve and unity shown by the American people in 1941 would be matched in 2001. Others wondered whether September 11 would become a defining experience for this current generation of Americans, much as Pearl Harbor had been for members of a previous generation. In attempting to answer these questions, it is instructive to note both the parallels and differences between the two events.

Casualties and perpetrators

Both Pearl Harbor and the September 11 attacks resulted in a large loss of human life. The attack on Pearl Harbor killed 2,388 people. The September 11 carnage was even larger, although an exact number was difficult to ascertain at first. In the initial weeks following September 11, the rough media consensus for the total number of fatalities at the WTC, the Pentagon, and in Pennsylvania was six or seven thousand (numbers cited by some of the articles in this volume). As weeks and months went by, that number consistently shrank, eventually reaching three thousand.

The September 11 casualties were not only numerically larger than those of Pearl Harbor, they were also different in nature. Pearl Harbor was a military attack against American military targets. Most of the casualties were sailors or soldiers; of the 2,388 people killed, forty-eight were civilians. For the most part, the September 11 attacks were directed not at soldiers or military targets, but at civilians going about their everyday jobs. For many, the fact that the September 11 terrorists targeted civilians made these acts even more outrageous and horrific than the events of 1941.

Another important difference between the two events was the identities of the attackers. On December 7, 1941, Americans knew who the enemy was—the Japanese Empire—and what its intentions were—to wage war against the United States. On September 11, 2001, Americans knew they had been attacked and perhaps were even at war, but they did not know who the enemy was or what their future intentions were.

In the days following September 11, 2001, some answers to these questions were found. Investigators from the Federal Bureau of Investigation (FBI) and other law enforcement agencies identified the nineteen air passengers that they believed were responsible for the attacks. The presumed terrorists were all men from Middle Eastern countries, including Egypt and Saudi Arabia. Suspicion quickly zeroed in on an organization called al-Qaida (the base), a terrorist network led by Osama bin Laden, a Saudi Arabian exile who had taken up residence in Afghanistan.

Thus, Americans were facing significantly different enemies in 1941 and 2001. Historian and World War II veteran Frank Mathias notes that Japan was a powerful nation with 191 infantry divisions and a large navy, as well as the support of Germany and Italy, while al-Qaida had "no navy, no organized army, no airforce." However, the absence of such resources did not prevent the shadowy terrorist organization from inflicting the damage of September 11.

America's response

In both 1941 and 2001, Americans responded quickly and patriotically, but were called upon to do different things. In 1941 Americans swamped military recruiting stations or waited for draft notices and sacrificed personal comforts for the war effort. In 2001 Americans expressed support for the paid professionals of the U.S. military and were called upon to spend the United States out of economic recession. Both eras were marked by upswings of patriotism and unity that extended to the federal government. Following the Pearl Harbor attacks, U.S. president Franklin D. Roosevelt addressed Congress and called for a declaration of war against Japan. Congress, previously divided and strongly isolationist, passed a war declaration with only one dissenting vote. Following the September 11 attacks, President George W. Bush addressed Congress, argued that the evidence pointed to al-Qaida, and called for a "war on terror" that "will not end until every terrorist group of global reach has been found, stopped, and defeated." He issued an ultimatum against the Taliban regime in Afghanistan, which he accused of harboring bin Laden and his network of terrorists. Congress, which earlier in 2001 had been preoccupied with domestic issues and partisan disputes, passed (again with one dissenting vote) a resolution authorizing Bush to use military force.

America's war against Japan in 1941 resulted in victory in 1945. America's war against terrorism is incomplete. On October 7, 2001, after marshaling diplomatic support worldwide, the United States began a bombing campaign in Afghanistan. By the end of 2001, Afghan rebels, assisted by U.S. bombing and special forces, had toppled the Taliban regime, and numerous al-Qaida officials were either killed or captured (Osama bin Laden himself, however, remained at large).

The successful yet inconclusive results of America's initial military campaign again highlight the differences between 1941 and 2001. America's war against Japan not only had a clear enemy, but a clear objective—Japan's defeat and official surrender. America's war against terrorism promised no such clear-cut solution. Even if Osama bin Laden were to be captured or killed, that would not necessarily signal the end of terrorism's threat to America. Bin Laden's followers and other terrorists hiding in nations such as Pakistan, Somalia, and the Philippines will likely prove to be elusive targets.

Patriotism and dissent

Both the Pearl Harbor and September 11 attacks resulted in an upsurge of patriotism. Following September 11, Americans purchased and proudly displayed the national flag. Hundreds of millions of dollars of charitable contributions flowed to organizations and individuals to help the families of those killed. Partisan differences in Washington were temporarily put aside to pass national security legislation. But the unity of spirit that the United States showed in the days, weeks, and months following September 11 did not necessarily translate into uniformity of opinion. Virtually all American and foreign observers condemned the actions as horrible and unjustified. Differences of opinion remained, however, on the difficult question of *why* these particular individuals did something so horrible (at the cost of their own lives).

Even commentators who see parallels between Pearl Harbor and September 11 disagree on the meaning of these events. Military historian Victor Davis Hanson writes that the lessons Americans learned from Pearl Harbor and September 11 are essentially the same: "There is no quarter to be given criminals, whether they be fascist states or murderous fundamentalists," and the American people, "self-absorbed" in times of peace, are quickly roused to eradicate enemies when attacked. Religious studies professor Ira Chernus, on the other hand, argues that just as Pearl Harbor needs to be seen in the context of American foreign policy in Asia, September 11 needs to be analyzed in light of U.S. actions in the Muslim world. He asserts that it is a "myth" that the United States was "naïve and innocent, isolated from the world" prior to Pearl Harbor and that the Japanese were simply "the devil incarnate" with "no possible rational motive" for attacking. It is a similar myth to portray the September 11 terrorists simply as "agents of the devil, doing evil for evil's sake, as if their own history and the world's history had nothing to do with it."

A point of agreement between Hanson and Chernus is that Americans cannot ignore events beyond their borders—in times of peace or war. The events of September 11, 2001, much as Pearl Harbor before it, will color how the United States interacts with the global community for years to come. The articles in this volume provide opinions and views on the causes, meaning, and potential consequences of the events of September 11, 2001, for the United States and the world.

1

Enemies of Freedom Committed an Act of War Against America

George W. Bush

George W. Bush is president of the United States. Nine days after the September 11, 2001, attack, he made this televised address to Congress and the American people.

The United States has been victimized by an act of war carried out by terrorists. Evidence indicates that the attack was organized and carried out by the al-Qaida [al Queda] terrorist network. This organization is led by Osama bin Laden, who is being sheltered by the Taliban government in Afghanistan. The enemies of freedom who have attacked America will not prevail. The spirit of the American people remains unbroken, and the United States will do whatever is necessary to defend itself against further attacks and to defeat and destroy global terrorists. The fight against terrorism is not just America's struggle, but one that calls on all civilized nations.

On September the 11th, enemies of freedom committed an act of war against our country. Americans have known wars—but for the past 136 years, they have been wars on foreign soil, except for one Sunday in 1941. Americans have known the casualties of war—but not at the center of a great city on a peaceful morning. Americans have known surprise attacks—but never before on thousands of civilians. All of this was brought upon us in a single day—and night fell on a different world, a world where freedom itself is under attack.

Americans have many questions tonight. Americans are asking: Who attacked our country? The evidence we have gathered all points to a collection of loosely affiliated terrorist organizations known as al Qaeda. They are the same murderers indicted for bombing American embassies in Tanzania and Kenya, and responsible for bombing the USS Cole.

Al Qaeda is to terror what the mafia is to crime. But its goal is not

Excerpted from George W. Bush's "Address to a Joint Session of Congress and the American People," September 20, 2001.

making money; its goal is remaking the world—and imposing its radical beliefs on people everywhere.

The terrorists practice a fringe form of Islamic extremism that has been rejected by Muslim scholars and the vast majority of Muslim clerics—a fringe movement that perverts the peaceful teachings of Islam. The terrorists' directive commands them to kill Christians and Jews, to kill all Americans, and make no distinction among military and civilians, including women and children.

This group and its leader—a person named Osama bin Laden—are linked to many other organizations in different countries, including the Egyptian Islamic Jihad and the Islamic Movement of Uzbekistan. There are thousands of these terrorists in more than 60 countries. They are recruited from their own nations and neighborhoods and brought to camps in places like Afghanistan, where they are trained in the tactics of terror. They are sent back to their homes or sent to hide in countries around the world to plot evil and destruction.

Al Qaeda and Afghanistan

The leadership of al Qaeda has great influence in Afghanistan and supports the Taliban regime in controlling most of that country. In Afghanistan, we see al Qaeda's vision for the world.

Afghanistan's people have been brutalized—many are starving and many have fled. Women are not allowed to attend school. You can be jailed for owning a television. Religion can be practiced only as their leaders dictate. A man can be jailed in Afghanistan if his beard is not long enough.

The United States respects the people of Afghanistan—after all, we are currently its largest source of humanitarian aid—but we condemn the Taliban regime. It is not only repressing its own people, it is threatening people everywhere by sponsoring and sheltering and supplying terrorists. By aiding and abetting murder, the Taliban regime is committing murder.

And tonight, the United States of America makes the following demands on the Taliban: Deliver to United States authorities all the leaders of al Qaeda who hide in your land. Release all foreign nationals, including American citizens, you have unjustly imprisoned. Protect foreign journalists, diplomats and aid workers in your country. Close immediately and permanently every terrorist training camp in Afghanistan, and hand over every terrorist, and every person in their support structure, to appropriate authorities. Give the United States full access to terrorist training camps, so we can make sure they are no longer operating.

These demands are not open to negotiation or discussion. The Taliban must act, and act immediately. They will hand over the terrorists, or they will share in their fate.

America's enemy

I also want to speak tonight directly to Muslims throughout the world. We respect your faith. It's practiced freely by many millions of Americans, and by millions more in countries that America counts as friends. Its teachings are good and peaceful, and those who commit evil in the name of Allah blaspheme the name of Allah. The terrorists are traitors to their own faith, trying, in effect, to hijack Islam itself. The enemy of America is not our many Muslim friends; it is not our many Arab friends. Our enemy is a radical network of terrorists, and every government that supports them.

Our war on terror begins with al Qaeda, but it does not end there. It will not end until every terrorist group of global reach has been found, stopped and defeated.

Americans are asking, why do they hate us? They hate what we see right here in this chamber—a democratically elected government. Their leaders are self-appointed. They hate our freedoms—our freedom of religion, our freedom of speech, our freedom to vote and assemble and disagree with each other.

They want to overthrow existing governments in many Muslim countries, such as Egypt, Saudi Arabia, and Jordan. They want to drive Israel out of the Middle East. They want to drive Christians and Jews out of vast regions of Asia and Africa.

On September the 11th, enemies of freedom committed an act of war against our country.

These terrorists kill not merely to end lives, but to disrupt and end a way of life. With every atrocity, they hope that America grows fearful, retreating from the world and forsaking our friends. They stand against us, because we stand in their way.

We are not deceived by their pretenses to piety. We have seen their kind before. They are the heirs of all the murderous ideologies of the 20th century. By sacrificing human life to serve their radical visions—by abandoning every value except the will to power—they follow in the path of fascism, and Nazism, and totalitarianism. And they will follow that path all the way, to where it ends: in history's unmarked grave of discarded lies.

The coming war

Americans are asking: How will we fight and win this war? We will direct every resource at our command—every means of diplomacy, every tool of intelligence, every instrument of law enforcement, every financial influence, and every necessary weapon of war—to the disruption and to the defeat of the global terror network.

This war will not be like the war against Iraq a decade ago, with a decisive liberation of territory and a swift conclusion. It will not look like the air war above Kosovo two years ago, where no ground troops were used and not a single American was lost in combat.

Our response involves far more than instant retaliation and isolated strikes. Americans should not expect one battle, but a lengthy campaign, unlike any other we have ever seen. It may include dramatic strikes, visible on TV, and covert operations, secret even in success. We will starve terrorists of funding, turn them one against another, drive them from place to place, until there is no refuge or no rest. And we will pursue nations that provide aid or safe haven to terrorism. Every nation, in every region, now has a decision to make. Either you are with us, or you are with the terrorists. From this day forward, any nation that continues to harbor or support terrorism will be regarded by the United States as a hostile regime.

Our nation has been put on notice: We are not immune from attack. We will take defensive measures against terrorism to protect Americans. Today, dozens of federal departments and agencies, as well as state and local governments, have responsibilities affecting homeland security. These efforts must be coordinated at the highest level. So tonight I announce the creation of a Cabinet-level position reporting directly to me— the Office of Homeland Security.

Our war on terror . . . will not end until every terrorist group of global reach has been found, stopped and defeated.

And tonight I also announce a distinguished American to lead this effort, to strengthen American security: a military veteran, an effective governor, a true patriot, a trusted friend—Pennsylvania's Tom Ridge. He will lead, oversee and coordinate a comprehensive national strategy to safeguard our country against terrorism, and respond to any attacks that may come.

These measures are essential. But the only way to defeat terrorism as a threat to our way of life is to stop it, eliminate it, and destroy it where it grows.

Many will be involved in this effort, from FBI agents to intelligence operatives to the reservists we have called to active duty. All deserve our thanks, and all have our prayers. And tonight, a few miles from the damaged Pentagon, I have a message for our military: Be ready. I've called the Armed Forces to alert, and there is a reason. The hour is coming when America will act, and you will make us proud.

Civilization's fight

This is not, however, just America's fight. And what is at stake is not just America's freedom. This is the world's fight. This is civilization's fight. This is the fight of all who believe in progress and pluralism, tolerance and freedom.

We ask every nation to join us. We will ask, and we will need, the help of police forces, intelligence services, and banking systems around the world. The United States is grateful that many nations and many international organizations have already responded—with sympathy and with support. Nations from Latin America, to Asia, to Africa, to Europe, to the Islamic world. Perhaps the NATO Charter reflects best the attitude of the world: An attack on one is an attack on all.

The civilized world is rallying to America's side. They understand that if this terror goes unpunished, their own cities, their own citizens may be next. Terror, unanswered, can not only bring down buildings, it can threaten the stability of legitimate governments. And you know what— we're not going to allow it.

What Americans must do

Americans are asking: What is expected of us? I ask you to live your lives, and hug your children. I know many citizens have fears tonight, and I ask you to be calm and resolute, even in the face of a continuing threat.

I ask you to uphold the values of America, and remember why so many have come here. We are in a fight for our principles, and our first responsibility is to live by them. No one should be singled out for unfair treatment or unkind words because of their ethnic background or religious faith.

I ask you to continue to support the victims of this tragedy with your contributions. Those who want to give can go to a central source of information, libertyunites.org, to find the names of groups providing direct help in New York, Pennsylvania, and Virginia.

The thousands of FBI agents who are now at work in this investigation may need your cooperation, and I ask you to give it.

I ask for your patience, with the delays and inconveniences that may accompany tighter security; and for your patience in what will be a long struggle.

What is at stake is not just America's freedom. This is the world's fight.

I ask your continued participation and confidence in the American economy. Terrorists attacked a symbol of American prosperity. They did not touch its source. America is successful because of the hard work, and creativity, and enterprise of our people. These were the true strengths of our economy before September 11th, and they are our strengths today.

And, finally, please continue praying for the victims of terror and their families, for those in uniform, and for our great country. Prayer has comforted us in sorrow, and will help strengthen us for the journey ahead.

New challenges

Tonight I thank my fellow Americans for what you have already done and for what you will do. And ladies and gentlemen of the Congress, I thank you, their representatives, for what you have already done and for what we will do together.

Tonight, we face new and sudden national challenges. We will come together to improve air safety, to dramatically expand the number of air marshals on domestic flights, and take new measures to prevent hijacking. We will come together to promote stability and keep our airlines flying, with direct assistance during this emergency.

We will come together to give law enforcement the additional tools it needs to track down terror here at home. We will come together to strengthen our intelligence capabilities to know the plans of terrorists before they act, and find them before they strike.

We will come together to take active steps that strengthen America's economy, and put our people back to work.

Tonight we welcome two leaders who embody the extraordinary

spirit of all New Yorkers: Governor George Pataki, and Mayor Rudolph Giuliani. As a symbol of America's resolve, my administration will work with Congress, and these two leaders, to show the world that we will rebuild New York City.

America's future

After all that has just passed—all the lives taken, and all the possibilities and hopes that died with them—it is natural to wonder if America's future is one of fear. Some speak of an age of terror. I know there are struggles ahead, and dangers to face. But this country will define our times, not be defined by them. As long as the United States of America is determined and strong, this will not be an age of terror; this will be an age of liberty, here and across the world.

Great harm has been done to us. We have suffered great loss. And in our grief and anger we have found our mission and our moment. Freedom and fear are at war. The advance of human freedom—the great achievement of our time, and the great hope of every time—now depends on us. Our nation—this generation—will lift a dark threat of violence from our people and our future. We will rally the world to this cause by our efforts, by our courage. We will not tire, we will not falter, and we will not fail.

It is my hope that in the months and years ahead, life will return almost to normal. We'll go back to our lives and routines, and that is good. Even grief recedes with time and grace. But our resolve must not pass. Each of us will remember what happened that day, and to whom it happened. We'll remember the moment the news came—where we were and what we were doing. Some will remember an image of a fire, or a story of rescue. Some will carry memories of a face and a voice gone forever.

And I will carry this: It is the police shield of a man named George Howard, who died at the World Trade Center trying to save others. It was given to me by his mom, Arlene, as a proud memorial to her son. This is my reminder of lives that ended, and a task that does not end.

I will not forget this wound to our country or those who inflicted it. I will not yield; I will not rest; I will not relent in waging this struggle for freedom and security for the American people.

The course of this conflict is not known, yet its outcome is certain. Freedom and fear, justice and cruelty, have always been at war, and we know that God is not neutral between them.

Fellow citizens, we'll meet violence with patient justice—assured of the rightness of our cause, and confident of the victories to come. In all that lies before us, may God grant us wisdom, and may He watch over the United States of America.

2

The Attacks Were God's Punishment for America's Actions Against Islam

Osama bin Laden

Osama bin Laden, a wealthy native of Saudi Arabia, is the head of al-Qaida ("The Base"), a terrorist network. Believed to be responsible for organizing two 1998 bombings of U.S. embassies in Africa, he was an immediate prime suspect for masterminding the September 11, 2001, attacks on America. The following is a translation of taped remarks that aired on an Arab television station on October 7. The remarks were first broadcast shortly after American and British forces began bombing operations that day in Afghanistan, where bin Laden has resided since 1996.

What America has experienced is God's just punishment for the sufferings they have inflicted on the world of Islam. It is good America is full of fear. The United States will not know peace until the infidels (Americans) leave the land of Muhammad (Saudi Arabia) and peace is secured in Palestine.

I bear witness that there is no God but Allah and that Mohammad is his messenger.

There is America, hit by God in one of its softest spots. Its greatest buildings were destroyed, thank God for that. There is America, full of fear from its north to its south, from its west to its east. Thank God for that.

What America is tasting now is something insignificant compared to what we have tasted for scores of years. Our nation (the Islamic world) has been tasting this humiliation and this degradation for more than 80 years. Its sons are killed, its blood is shed, its sanctuaries are attacked, and no one hears and no one heeds.

When God blessed one of the groups of Islam, vanguards of Islam, they destroyed America. I pray to God to elevate their status and bless them.

Millions of innocent children are being killed as I speak. They are being killed in Iraq without committing any sins, and we don't hear condemnation or a fatwa (religious decree) from the rulers. In these days, Israeli tanks infest Palestine—in Jenin, Ramallah, Rafah, Beit Jalla, and other places in the land of Islam, and we don't hear anyone raising his voice or moving a limb.

American hypocrisy

When the sword comes down (on America), after 80 years, hypocrisy rears its ugly head. They deplore and they lament for those killers, who have abused the blood, honor and sanctuaries of Muslims. The least that can be said about those people is that they are debauched. They have followed injustice. They supported the butcher over the victim, the oppressor over the innocent child. May God show them His wrath and give them what they deserve.

I say that the situation is clear and obvious. After this event, after the senior officials have spoken in America, starting with the head of infidels worldwide, Bush, and those with him. They have come out in force with their men and have turned even the countries that belong to Islam to this treachery, and they want to wag their tail at God, to fight Islam, to suppress people in the name of terrorism.

What America is tasting now is something insignificant compared to what we have tasted for scores of years.

When people at the ends of the earth, Japan, were killed by their hundreds of thousands, young and old, it was not considered a war crime, it is something that has justification. Millions of children in Iraq is something that has justification. But when they lose dozens of people in Nairobi and Dar es Salaam (capitals of Kenya and Tanzania, where U.S. embassies were bombed in 1998), Iraq was struck and Afghanistan was struck. Hypocrisy stood in force behind the head of infidels worldwide, behind the cowards of this age, America and those who are with it.

These events have divided the whole world into two sides. The side of believers and the side of infidels, may God keep you away from them. Every Muslim has to rush to make his religion victorious. The winds of faith have come. The winds of change have come to eradicate oppression from the island of Muhammad, peace be upon him.

To America, I say only a few words to it and its people. I swear by God, who has elevated the skies without pillars, neither America nor the people who live in it will dream of security before we live it in Palestine, and not before all the infidel armies leave the land of Muhammad, peace be upon him.

God is great, may pride be with Islam. May peace and God's mercy be upon you.

3

Osama bin Laden Wants to Drive the West from the Islamic World

James S. Robbins

James S. Robbins is an international relations professor at National Defense University.

Osama bin Laden's statement released on October 7, 2001, reveals some clues as to his motives behind his endorsement and alleged planning of the World Trade Center and Pentagon terrorist attacks. He wishes to rid the Middle East of Western influence and to overthrow regimes in Saudi Arabia and Jordan that trace their roots to post–World War I European diplomacy. His comments calling on Muslims everywhere to resist the United States reveal that America's war against terrorism is not against one man or regime, but against an ideology that is diametrically opposed to the American way of life.

Osama bin Laden's statement Sunday [October 7, 2001] after the first Allied air strikes in Afghanistan was mostly what one would expect, the usual denunciations of the United States and "the chief infidel Bush," but did contain two curious passages: "Our nation has undergone more than 80 years of this humiliation . . ."; and: "When the sword reached America after 80 years . . ." Eighty years? 1921? Is he saying that this whole thing is Warren G. Harding's fault?

Bin Laden is talking about the 1920 Treaty of Sèvres imposed on the Turks after World War One, which detached their Arab provinces and spelled the end of the Ottoman Empire. The Ottomans had ruled the region for 600 years or so, and brought varying degrees of political harmony under the Sultanate and religious unity under the Caliphate [Islamic realm ruled by the caliphs, successors to Mohammad]. The 1920 treaty did away with the political order, and the Caliphate was banned by Kemal Ataturk in 1924. The European powers saw to the disposition of the Arab lands, the route to British India was secured from Russian expansionism, France was given an interest in Syria, and the Mideast oil supplies were safe.

Old news? Well, we are dealing with people with long historical memory. Ayman Zawahri, leader of the Egyptian Jihad, stated on October 7 that his group "will not tolerate a recurrence of the Andalusia tragedy in Palestine." (The Andalusia tragedy is the end of Moorish rule in Spain in 1492.)

So the World Trade Towers had to come down because some psychopath can't come to grips with the end of World War I? Basically, yes. In bin Laden's universe, that was when everything started to go wrong. Viewed in that context, his plots against the Saudi and Jordanian monarchies make perfect sense. They are products of this original sin, the establishment of the political order of the Middle East by the Allied powers 80 years ago. The founding of Israel ("the Zionist entity") is an echo of the same Western interference. Iraq's annexation of Kuwait in 1991 was an attempt to right things—Kuwait was part of the same administrative division as Iraq within the Ottoman Empire, so it is only just that it be reclaimed. Hence, Western opposition to Saddam's invasion is a key event to bin Laden. He mentions this specifically in his 1998 *fatwa* [decree issued by an Islamic religious leader] against Americans, and also in his most recent statement in which he says there will be no peace until, among other things, "and all infidel armies depart from the land of Mohammad," i.e., Americans leave Saudi Arabia.

Comprehending our enemy

It is important to understand these dates and events to comprehend the adversary we face. Bin Laden looks back to what he believes was a golden age in which Western influence in the Mideast was minimal and there was no interference in Muslim affairs by "atheists." If he and his followers could recreate that environment, they could construct a theocratic utopia after the blueprint of Taliban Afghanistan. The main impediments to that vision are the Arab monarchies and autocracies that do business with the west. Bin Laden must first drive out the infidels who prop up these regimes, then topple them and replace them with pure Islamic states (that is, Islam *ala* Osama).

> *Bin Laden looks back to what he believes was a golden age in which Western influence in the Mideast was minimal.*

Those who see poverty at the root of all conflict should note well that Osama bin Laden and the members of Al Qaeda are the products of affluence. The September 11 suicide hijackers were more familiar with the discos of Berlin than the slums of Ramallah. We are not dealing with politicians who can be bought off with an increased minimum wage and comprehensive national health care plan. These are idealists violently promoting a comprehensive and exclusive worldview. Bin Laden said Sunday, "These events have divided the world into two parts: a part that espouses faith and is devoid of hypocrisy, and an infidel part, may God protect us from it." As an Al Qaeda spokesman put it, "There are only two sides and no third one. Either you chose the side of faith or that of atheism." There can be no compromise; this is war to the death.

The scope of the current war is vast. It is not a struggle against one demented man, or one radical regime. It is a war against an idea, an ideology antithetical to our way of life and to the western conception of freedom. Afghanistan is the nerve center of this ideology, a state that has supplied safe haven to its theorists, and a test bed for its practitioners. But the tendrils of this network reach far; to Indonesia, the Philippines, western China, Chechnya, the Balkans, Nigeria, and Colombia to name a few. It is a global web tied to organized crime, narcotics, and arms smuggling. Its lifeblood is money, much of which is obtained through illegal activity. But it also does commerce in mercenaries, and supplies tactical training and ideological indoctrination. This is not the type of threat our national-security apparatus is organized to defeat, but it is the one with which we must now come to grips.

New strategies

The United States doesn't formulate 80- or even eight-year strategies. Our approach to problems is to wait until they get serious, go in, fix them, and leave. We thought we did this in Iraq in 1991; clearly we did not. Likewise with Afghanistan—after Soviet forces withdrew in 1989 we were done with that country and let it fall into chaos. We figured our friends the Pakistanis would take care of it, and they certainly did. Their answer was the Taliban, which gave Afghanistan more stability than it had seen in years. True, it was the stability of the graveyard, but that served Pakistan's interests. And when it became clear that serious problems were developing in Afghanistan, the Clinton administration responded by placing sanctions on Pakistan for engaging in nuclear testing and feebly launching cruise missiles into the Afghan mountains. The single most significant diplomatic move in the current conflict was lifting the sanctions and detaching Pakistan from the Taliban. The Afghan regime has no hope of survival without its Pakistani patrons, and without the Taliban the Al Qaeda network has no cover. One hopes that when the smoke clears and Afghanistan is liberated the United States will not revert to its traditional regional attention deficit disorder.

The opening shots of this war were not fired October 7, but the instant President Bush responded on September 11. The United States is now formulating a new type of warfighting strategy. Military force is a necessary and powerful part of the solution, but there are important roles to be played by law enforcement, intelligence, diplomacy, international financial agreements, covert operations, foreign aid—almost every tool at the disposal of the government must be utilized to win this struggle. It will take time, steady leadership, and strategic vision. Bin Laden may die tomorrow—*inshallah* [if Allah wills]—but we have a long way to go.

4

The Attacks Were Part of Militant Islam's War Against America

Daniel Pipes

Daniel Pipes is the director of the Middle East Forum, a think tank that works to define and promote American interests in the Middle East. He is the author of numerous books and articles on the region.

The September 11, 2001, terrorist attacks against the World Trade Center towers and the Pentagon were the latest in a long series of actions that comprise militant Islam's war against the United States. Previous attacks include 1983 bombings against the U.S. embassy and marine barracks in Lebanon, bombings of embassies in Africa, and killings of Americans in New York and other places. Future attacks by militant Islamists may be even worse, involving weapons of mass destruction.

All four of the plane crashes on September 11 occurred in the northeastern United States, where I live. According to the latest *Newsweek* poll, a massive two-thirds of my neighbors feel "less safe" than they did before that day.

I beg to disagree. This particular American now feels more secure. The reason? Those terrible events alerted my fellow citizens to the fact that militant Islam is engaged in fighting a war on the United States.

War began in 1979

That war began, not as people seem to think, in September 2001 but in February 1979, when Ayatollah Khomeini took power in Iran. Already by November 1979, Khomeini had seized the US Embassy in Teheran and held nearly 60 captives for 444 days. Eight American soldiers (the first casualties in this war) died in the failed US rescue attempt in 1980.

The Islamists' initial major act of violence against Americans, killing 63, took place in 1983 when they attacked the US Embassy in Beirut. As the analyst David Makovsky notes, Washington "beat a hasty exit, and Islamic militants saw this as a vindication that suicide bombing was . . . deadly effective." Then followed a rapid sequence of attacks on Americans in Lebanon (the embassy a second time, a Marine barracks, airline passengers, university presidents), plus other Middle Eastern countries.

This assault persisted for the next 18 years. Prominent targets included American soldiers in Saudi Arabia (twice), two embassies in East Africa, and a warship in Yemen. Further afield, Islamists killed Americans in Israel, Pakistan, Kashmir, and the Philippines.

Militant Islam seeks to destroy the United States.

Attacks on US soil began with the 1980 murder of an anti-Khomeini Iranian resident in the Washington, DC, area. Subsequent killings included a Muslim religious figure in Tucson, Arizona, a Jewish leader in New York City, and CIA employees waiting in their cars to enter the agency headquarters. A rash of murders took place at New York landmarks—the World Trade Center, the Brooklyn Bridge, the Empire State Building.

Washington threatened retribution ("You can run but you can't hide") for attacks against Americans, but hardly ever carried through. Rather, the preferred US response was to hunker down behind concrete barriers, thick walls, and security checks. Intelligence and defense capabilities remained inadequate. Actual perpetrators were sometimes caught and tried in court, but the apparatus that trained and dispatched them remained unscathed.

America awakes

The sad fact is, 22 years and 600 dead did not get the country's attention. Americans blithely ignored those specialists on militant Islam and terrorism who pleaded for vigilance and warned of horrors to come. This national obliviousness explains how Americans found themselves so embarrassingly unprepared for the events of September 11. "Scandal" is how one Israeli pilot correctly describes the military's inability to protect the World Trade Center or the Pentagon.

Nearly 7,000 deaths in one day did, at least, finally awake the country.

And I feel safer now, as the FBI is engaged in the largest operation in its history, armed marshals will again be flying on US aircraft, and the immigration service has placed foreign students under increased scrutiny. I feel safer when Islamist organizations are exposed, illicit money channels closed down, and immigration regulations reviewed. The amassing of American forces near Iraq and Afghanistan cheers me. The newfound alarm is healthy, the sense of solidarity heartening, the resolve is encouraging.

But will it last? Are Americans truly ready to sacrifice liberties and lives to prosecute seriously the war against militant Islam? I worry about US constancy and purpose.

One thing is very sure: should the thousands of deaths of fellow citizens not inspire Americans to extirpate the threat of militant Islam, then this will be back, and more dangerous next time. September's carnage was limited to the destruction of things crashing into each other, but future Islamist attacks are likely to involve weapons of mass destruction. Should that happen, the death toll could be in the millions, not the thousands.

So, let this warning be clear: Militant Islam seeks to destroy the United States (as well as Europe, Israel, and many other societies) as presently constituted. Islamists have shown resolve, tenacity, and tactical brilliance. Unless Westerners take this threat very much to heart, Islamists will be back, dispensing far worse punishments.

5

The Terrorist Attacks
Were Not the Result
of U.S. Actions

Peter Beinart

Peter Beinart is editor of the New Republic, *a weekly journal of opinion.*

Some people have blamed the September 11 terrorist attacks on "blowback"—the unintended consequences of U.S. foreign policy actions. They have argued that the rise of Osama bin Laden, believed to be the mastermind behind the attacks, was in part the result of American intervention in the war between Afghanistan and the Soviet Union in the 1980s. But a careful reading of history indicates otherwise. Bin Laden's rise is attributable to America's disengagement from Afghanistan, not its intervention there.

When America goes to war, Americans ask a historical question: How did we get ourselves into this? Doves usually answer: imperialism. If we didn't do such nasty things around the world, we wouldn't be attacked. But the connection between our misdeeds and their attacks can be rather tenuous. And so more sophisticated doves offer a more sophisticated answer: "blowback." Our foreign policy doesn't just create enemies in a general sense, it creates them in a very specific sense: We fund and train the people who later attack us. During the Panama invasion, doves gleefully noted Manuel Noriega's ties to the CIA. During the Gulf war [against Iraq], they gleefully noted America's semi-support for Saddam [Hussein] as a counterweight to Iran. And today antiwar commentators instruct us that the CIA, through its support for the Afghan war against the Soviet Union, created Osama bin Laden.

At first glance, blowback might not seem like a good historical argument for doves to make. After all, by condemning the U.S. for getting into bed with Noriega and Saddam and bin Laden in the past, doves acknowledge that they are worthy of condemnation—which might suggest that America should atone for its past wrongs by opposing them now. But doves aren't making a point about America's enemies; they are making a point about America. The assumption behind blowback is that the U.S. *can't* atone—that as long as it intervenes around the world, it will foster evil. To go to war against bin Laden today will only create more bin Ladens tomorrow.

The case of Afghanistan

Which makes it of more than mere historical interest that, as applied to the United States and Afghanistan, the blowback theory is dead wrong. American intervention in the Afghan war didn't create Osama bin Laden. In fact, if the United States bears any blame for bin Laden's terrorist network today, it's because in the 1980s and '90s, we didn't intervene in Afghanistan aggressively *enough*.

As bizarre as it may sound to the antiwar left, the CIA was deeply wary of U.S. involvement in Afghanistan. The Agency didn't think the mujahedin rebels could beat Moscow, and it feared that if it ran the war, it would take the blame if things went awry. As Vincent Cannistraro, who led the Reagan administration's Afghan Working Group from 1985 to 1987, puts it, "The CIA was very reluctant to be involved at all. They thought it would end up with them being blamed, like in Guatemala." So the Agency tried to avoid direct involvement in the war, and to maintain plausible deniability. For the first six years following the 1979 Soviet invasion, the U.S. provided the mujahedin only Eastern-bloc weaponry, so the rebels could claim they had captured it from Soviet troops rather than received it from Washington. And while America funded the mujahedin, it played barely any role in their training. To insulate itself, the U.S. gave virtual carte blanche to its allies, Pakistan and Saudi Arabia, to direct the rebel effort as they saw fit.

> *American intervention in the Afghan war didn't create Osama bin Laden.*

This is where bin Laden comes in. After Moscow invaded, he and other Arab militants went to defend Afghanistan in the name of Islam. The Pakistani government allowed them in, and the Saudis gave them money, hoping to foster a Sunni Islamist network to counter the Shia network of rival Iran. Riyadh thought the network would espouse the monarchy's brand of conservative, rather than revolutionary, fundamentalism. And that idea seemed less naive in the 1980s when bin Laden was still a loyal Saudi subject, and before Islamist rebellions had broken out in Algeria and dramatically intensified in Egypt.

Had the U.S. been present on the ground in Afghanistan, it would have known about this. And it probably would have tried to stop it—if only because the Arab volunteers were aiding a virulently anti-Western Afghan rebel leader named Abdul Rasul Sayyaf, who opposed not only the Soviets, but the Western-backed mujahedin as well. But the U.S. wasn't present on the ground, and it had only the vaguest knowledge of the Arabs' presence and aims. In retrospect, that might seem hard to believe. But remember, contrary to bin Laden's later boasts, the Arabs were few in

number (most came *after* the war, once bin Laden's network was established) and played virtually no military role in the victory over the Soviets. And the skittish CIA, Cannistraro estimates, had less than ten operatives acting as America's eyes and ears in the region. Milton Bearden, the
Agency's chief field operative in the war effort, has insisted that "[T]he
CIA had nothing to do with" bin Laden. Cannistraro says that when he
coordinated Afghan policy from Washington, he never once heard bin
Laden's name.

U.S. disengagement

And if U.S. disengagement contributed to the formation of bin Laden's network during the war, it contributed to it after the war was over as well. In
1992 the Communist regime in Kabul finally fell. Afghanistan needed foreign aid to reconstruct its shattered infrastructure, and an intense diplomatic effort to force its fractious mujahedin leaders to lay down their arms.
The logical source of that financial assistance and political intervention was
the U.S., which enjoyed the goodwill of many mujahedin leaders. But by
all accounts, once Afghanistan's troubles lost their cold war significance,
the [George H.] Bush and Clinton administrations paid them virtually no
high-level attention. Neither administration tried seriously to negotiate a
truce between the parties, and U.S. aid, which had totaled roughly $3 bil-
lion in the 1980s, dropped, by the end of 1994, nearly to zero.

For two more hideous years, mujahedin factions fought each other and
preyed on an already brutalized population. Had ordinary Afghans not been
desperate for the civil war to end, and for a leadership with at least some
moral code, they would not have backed the Taliban, the religious students
coming from the Pakistani border. And had Afghanistan not faced a political vacuum, Pakistan would not have armed those students in the hope that
through them, it could dominate its neighbor to the northwest.

America's abandonment of Afghanistan was of a piece with its abandonment of countries like Liberia, Somalia, and Congo, which also disin-
tegrated after cold war dictators fell. In Liberia the resulting anarchy produced the murderous Charles Taylor. In Somalia it produced the
murderous Mohamed Farah Aideed. In Congo it produced the genocidal
Hutu refugee camps. And in Afghanistan it produced the Taliban. Except
that the Taliban didn't just harbor tribal killers, they harbored Al Qaeda,
which brought its savagery all the way to America's shores.

No blowback

So the doves are wrong. There was no blowback. America's involvement
in Afghanistan in the 1980s didn't help create Osama bin Laden; Saudi
Arabia's involvement in Afghanistan in the 1980s helped create Osama
bin Laden, in large part because the United States was too timid to direct
the war itself. Similarly, it wasn't America's intervention in Afghanistan
in the 1990s that created the Taliban; it was Pakistan's intervention and
America's non-intervention. Doves might consider this as they counsel
the U.S. to respond to September 11 by leaving the rest of the world to its
own devices. After all, it was leaving the rest of the world to its own devices that got us into this in the first place.

6

U.S. Policies in Islamic Lands Are a Root Cause of the Terrorist Attacks

Faisal Bodi

Faisal Bodi is a British Muslim writer.

In asking the question of why they were the target of terrorists, Americans must look at U.S. policies in the Middle East. By supporting totalitarian regimes in Middle East nations, imposing economic sanctions on Iraq, and supporting Israel against the Palestinian people, the United States has contributed to the deaths of many innocent people and has become a symbol of terror and oppression for many Muslims. The September 11, 2001, terrorist attacks were in part a result of American abuses of human rights abroad.

As Americans wake from the nightmare of September 11th's onslaught against their key commercial and political buildings, two questions are likely to be on their lips: who and why?

The who is the easy part. Only a well-financed, well-oiled and militarily sophisticated body could pull off such an audacious assault against a world superpower. All fingers point in one direction, to the mountains of Afghanistan where Osama bin Laden, multimillionaire and the leader of the international Muslim army, called al-Qaeda, has his lair.

Why is America a target?

The harder and more crucial question is why. Why does the US continue to be a target for Islamist attacks? The US marine barracks in Beirut in 1983, the World Trade Centre in 1993, the al-Khobar bombings in 1996, the USS Cole bombing in 2000, what is it about the US that makes it a magnet for Muslim militants?

President Bush and secretary of state Colin Powell gave their own take September 11. They blamed extremists bent on damaging democracy and western civilisation. Disturbingly, their views will likely wash with an audience whose grasp of international affairs is so dumbed down as to prevent them separating loaded representation from reality.

But much as the attacks on civilian structures might suggest otherwise, democracy is not the intended target here, and neither is freedom. Inside America, the Trade Centre, the Pentagon, Camp David, and Capitol Hill are all seen as symbols of global US power and prestige, of the triumph of democracy. Outside, in the Muslim world, they are popularly regarded as symbols of terror and oppression.

If the dark cloud of Muslim terrorism has a silver lining one prays it is an internal review of US foreign policy.

Since 1991, American-led sanctions against Iraq and the effects of depleted uranium have killed 1 million children. Who knows if the attackers intended all flights inside the US to come to a halt, but for a day at least they succeeded in turning the tables on the no-fly zone in force over Iraq. Since the Palestinian uprising started in September 2000, American Apache helicopters, F-16s and M-16 rifles have been responsible for killing 700 Palestinians and injuring 25,000 more. Since CNN isn't there, by design rather than accident, to capture every smashed skull and charred corpse, westerners remain ignorant of US terrorism.

These are only the more visible examples of US abuses in Muslim lands. As it waves the flag of democracy in one hand, Washington pours billions of dollars into upholding totalitarian regimes in Egypt, Jordan, Saudi Arabia, Algeria, among others, to make sure its people are prevented from exercising their collective will. The US Fifth Fleet sails menacingly around the Gulf in a warning to dissidents that it will use force to protect its client rulers and an uninterrupted supply of oil. And the presence of US troops in Saudi Arabia cocks a snook at Muslim sensibilities about their holy places.

Support for Israel

But it is the unqualified US support for Israel that most enrages Muslims. Camp David [the rumored target of the fourth hijacked plane] was no random choice. The site of the first peace agreement between a Muslim state [Egypt] and Israel in 1978, is still seen by many as a capitulation and a sell-out of the Palestinians. Official US aid to Israel in 2001 amounts to a non-repayable $6 billion. In September 2001 Israel announced it was to exercise an option to buy 50 more F-16s in order to keep up its military superiority over all its Arab neighbours. That it is almost exclusively the US in the firing line and not other western countries suggests that for the militants, silence in the continued oppression of the Palestinians is excusable, direct complicity is not.

It is unlikely this will happen, but if the dark cloud of Muslim terrorism has a silver lining one prays it is an internal review of US foreign policy, especially with regards to Israel. Yesterday's attacks are the chickens of America's callous abuse of others' human rights coming home to roost.

Though it is a minority view in Islam that countenances retaliatory attacks on civilians, it is one that US policy is encouraging. Terrorism begets terrorism. This is not to excuse the perpetrators but to offer a way out of the spiral of tit for tat terror.

But if previous bombings have not shocked the US into self-reflection it is unlikely that even this, the biggest attack on its shores since Pearl Harbour, will do so. The likelihood is that Washington will order its spin doctors to steer the public gaze well away from itself and towards intensified military efforts to snuff out Bin Laden. That would be the most terrifying outcome of all. One living Bin Laden is better than a martyr who spawns a hundred more.

7

The Terrorists Were Waging a War the United States Began

Samuel Francis

Samuel Francis is a conservative syndicated columnist.

Most media accounts and editorials have described the September 11 attacks as acts of war against the United States. The truth that has been obscured in media coverage is that the United States has already been at war with Middle East nations and organizations for years, dating back at least to 1991 when America launched and led a war against Iraq. That war and subsequent economic sanctions have killed thousands of civilians. In addition, former president Bill Clinton launched bombing and missile raids against civilians in the Middle East and Afghanistan to deflect attention from his domestic scandals. The attacks on Washington and New York were payback for American actions.

"We're at war," the young waitress, her voice catching, informed me when I first heard of the terrorist attacks on the World Trade Center and the Pentagon this week.

She was hardly the only one. "America at War," the *Washington Times'* lead editorial pronounced the next day. "It's WAR," screamed its editorial cartoon. A "new kind of war has been declared on the world's democracies," the *Wall Street Journal's* editorial pontificated. "The War Against America" was the subject of the *New York Times* editorial. "A state of war," the *Washington Post* called it. "This is war," pronounced columnist Charles Krauthammer. "They were acts of war," confirmed the president of the United States.

Well, it probably is—except that, even as everyone from waitresses to the president was declaring war or howling for it, nobody was exactly sure who we were at war with.

The usual suspect was the shadowy Osama bin Laden, though some experts said the attacks didn't fit his profile, and even if we were sure, no one seemed able to say how we should wage the war, how we could win it or what would constitute victory. Mainly, what most Americans wanted to do—entirely understandably—was to blow the hell out of somebody or something. No doubt, in time, we will.

A U.S. war

But the blunt truth is that the United States has been at war for years—at least a decade, since we launched a war against Iraq in 1991, even though Iraq had done absolutely nothing to harm the United States or any American. Our bombing attacks on Iraq certainly caused civilian casualties, and if they were not deliberate, nobody beating the war drums at the time felt much regret for them.

The terrorists attacked us because they were paying us back for what we started.

For 10 years, we have maintained economic sanctions on Iraq that have led to the deaths of hundreds of thousands of civilians, and we have repeatedly bombed it whenever it failed to abide by standards we imposed on it.

Under Bill Clinton, we again launched bombing raids against civilians—once against so-called "terrorist training camps" supposedly under bin Laden's control in Afghanistan and at the same time against a purported "chemical weapons factory" in Sudan that almost certainly was no such thing. The attacks just happened to occur on the same day as Monica Lewinsky's grand jury testimony that she had engaged in sex with the president. [In 1998 Clinton was embroiled in a sex scandal involving Lewinsky, an intern, and testimony regarding a sexual harassment suit by Arkansas state employee Paula Jones; the scandal eventually led to his impeachment.]

"This is unfortunately the war of the future," Secretary of State Madeleine Albright said in justifying the U.S. raids, officially launched in retaliation for terrorist attacks on American embassies.

Later the same year [1998], Clinton ordered (but later countermanded) yet more missile attacks on Iraq—the day after the Paula Jones sex scandal was settled in court. Later yet again, Clinton ordered more bombings in Iraq the day before Congress was scheduled to vote on his impeachment. Then there are the Balkans, where the United States has waddled forth to war for no compelling reason and where it has also slaughtered civilians with its unprovoked bombings.

Why terrorists attack

In all the buckets of media gabble about the terrorist attacks in New York and Washington, not once have I heard any journalist ask any expert the simple question, "Why did the terrorists attack us?"

There is, of course, an implicit answer to the unasked question: It's because the terrorists are "evil"; they "hate democracy"; they are "fanatics," "barbarians" and "cowards." Those, of course, are answers that can satisfy only children. Some day it might actually dawn on someone in this country that the grown-up but unwelcome answer is that the terrorists attacked us because they were paying us back for what we started.

Let us hear no more about how the "terrorists" have "declared war on America." Any nation that allows a criminal chief executive to use its military power to slaughter civilians in unprovoked and legally unauthorized attacks for his own personal political purposes can expect whatever the "terrorists" dish out to it. If, as President Bush told us, we should make no distinction between those who harbor terrorists and those who commit terrorist acts, neither can any distinction be made between those who tolerate the murderous policies of a criminal in power and the criminal himself.

The blunt and quite ugly truth is that the United States has been at war for years—that it started the war in the name of "spreading democracy," "building nations," "waging peace," "stopping aggression," "enforcing human rights" and all the other pious lies that warmongers always invoke to mask the truth, and that it continued the war simply to save a crook from political ruin.

What is new is merely that in September 2001, for the first time, the war we started came home—and all of a sudden, Americans don't seem to care for it so much.

8

"Blowback" from U.S. Foreign Policy Is Partially to Blame for the Attacks

Chalmers Johnson

Chalmers Johnson is the author of a dozen books concerning East Asia and political violence, including Revolutionary Change *and* Blowback: The Costs and Consequences of American Empire.

The terrorist attacks against the World Trade Center and the Pentagon were an example of "blowback"—a term created by the Central Intelligence Agency (CIA) to describe unintended consequences of U.S. activities abroad. Terrorist network leader Osama bin Laden was in part the creation of the United States, which funded his efforts against the Soviet Union in the 1980s. Rather than continue with foreign policy as usual, the United States needs to make a serious effort to analyze and curb its global military activities.

For Americans who can bear to think about it, those tragic pictures from New York of women holding up photos of their husbands, sons and daughters and asking if anyone knows anything about them look familiar. They are similar to scenes we have seen from Buenos Aires and Santiago. There, too, starting in the 1970s, women held up photos of their loved ones, asking for information. Since it was far too dangerous then to say aloud what they thought had happened to them—that they had been tortured and murdered by US-backed military juntas—the women coined a new word for them, *los desaparecidos*—"the disappeareds." Our government has never been honest about its own role in the 1973 overthrow of the elected government of Salvador Allende in Chile or its backing, through "Operation Condor," of what the State Department has recently called "extrajudicial killings" in Argentina, Paraguay, Brazil and elsewhere in Latin America. But we now have several thousand of our own disappeareds, and we are badly mistaken if we think that we in the United States are entirely blameless for what happened to them.

The suicidal assassins of September 11, 2001, did not "attack America," as our political leaders and the news media like to maintain; they attacked American foreign policy. Employing the strategy of the weak, they killed innocent bystanders who then became enemies only because they had already become victims. Terrorism by definition strikes at the innocent in order to draw attention to the sins of the invulnerable. The United States deploys such overwhelming military force globally that for its militarized opponents only an "asymmetric strategy," in the jargon of the Pentagon, has any chance of success. When it does succeed, as it did spectacularly on September 11, it renders our massive military machine worthless: The terrorists offer it no targets. On the day of the disaster, President George W. Bush told the American people that we were attacked because we are "a beacon for freedom" and because the attackers were "evil." In his address to Congress on September 20, he said, "This is civilization's fight." This attempt to define difficult-to-grasp events as only a conflict over abstract values—as a "clash of civilizations," in current post-cold war American jargon—is not only disingenuous but also a way of evading responsibility for the "blowback" that America's imperial projects have generated.

Unintended consequences

"Blowback" is a CIA term first used in March 1954 in a recently declassified report on the 1953 operation to overthrow the government of Mohammed Mossadegh in Iran. It is a metaphor for the unintended consequences of the US government's international activities that have been kept secret from the American people. The CIA's fears that there might ultimately be some blowback from its egregious interference in the affairs of Iran were well founded. Installing the Shah in power brought twenty-five years of tyranny and repression to the Iranian people and elicited the Ayatollah Khomeini's revolution. The staff of the American embassy in Teheran was held hostage for more than a year. This misguided "covert operation" of the US government helped convince many capable people throughout the Islamic world that the United States was an implacable enemy.

> *Osama bin Laden . . . is no more (or less) "evil" than his fellow creations of our CIA.*

The pattern has become all too familiar. Osama bin Laden, the leading suspect as mastermind behind the carnage of September 11, is no more (or less) "evil" than his fellow creations of our CIA: Manuel Noriega, former commander of the Panama Defense Forces until George H. Bush in late 1989 invaded his country and kidnapped him, or Iraq's Saddam Hussein, whom we armed and backed so long as he was at war with Khomeini's Iran and whose people we have bombed and starved for a decade in an incompetent effort to get rid of him. These men were once listed as "assets" of our clandestine services organization.

Osama bin Laden joined our call for resistance to the Soviet Union's

1979 invasion of Afghanistan and accepted our military training and equipment along with countless other mujahedeen "freedom fighters." It was only after the Russians bombed Afghanistan back into the stone age and suffered a Vietnam-like defeat, and we turned our backs on the death and destruction we had helped cause, that he turned against us. The last straw as far as bin Laden was concerned was that, after the Gulf War, we based "infidel" American troops in Saudi Arabia to prop up its decadent, fiercely authoritarian regime. Ever since, bin Laden has been attempting to bring the things the CIA taught him home to the teachers. On September 11, he appears to have returned to his deadly project with a vengeance.

Globalization and America

There are today, ten years after the demise of the Soviet Union, some 800 Defense Department installations located in other countries. The people of the United States make up perhaps 4 percent of the world's population but consume 40 percent of its resources. They exercise hegemony over the world directly through overwhelming military might and indirectly through secretive organizations like the World Bank, the International Monetary Fund and the World Trade Organization. Though largely dominated by the US government, these are formally international organizations and therefore beyond Congressional oversight.

As the American-inspired process of "globalization" inexorably enlarges the gap between the rich and the poor, a popular movement against it has gained strength, advancing from its first demonstrations in Seattle in 1999 through protests in Washington, DC; Melbourne; Prague; Seoul; Nice; Barcelona; Quebec City; Göteborg; and on to its violent confrontations in Genoa earlier this year [2001]. Ironically, though American leaders are deaf to the desires of the protesters, the Defense Department has actually adopted the movement's main premise—that current global economic arrangements mean more wealth for the "West" and more misery for the "rest"—as a reason why the United States should place weapons in space. The US Space Command's pamphlet "Vision for 2020" argues that "the globalization of the world economy will also continue, with a widening between the 'haves' and the 'have-nots,'" and that we have a mission to "dominate the space dimension of military operations to protect US interests and investments" in an increasingly dangerous and implicitly anti-American world. Unfortunately, while the eyes of military planners were firmly focused on the "control and domination" of space and "denying other countries access to space," a very different kind of space was suddenly occupied.

On the day after the September 11 attack, Democratic Senator Zell Miller of Georgia declared, "I say, bomb the hell out of them. If there's collateral damage, so be it." "Collateral damage" is another of those hateful euphemisms invented by our military to prettify its killing of the defenseless. It is the term Pentagon spokesmen use to refer to the Serb and Iraqi civilians who were killed or maimed by bombs from high-flying American warplanes in our campaigns against Slobodan Milosevic and Saddam Hussein. It is the kind of word our new ambassador to the United Nations, John Negroponte, might have used in the 1980s to explain the slaughter of peasants, Indians and church workers by American-backed right-wing death squads in El Salvador, Guatemala, Honduras and Nicaragua while he was ambassador to Honduras. These activities made the Reagan years the worst decade for Central America since the Spanish conquest.

Massive military retaliation with its inevitable "collateral damage" will, of course, create more desperate and embittered childless parents and parentless children, and so recruit more maddened people to the terrorists' cause. In fact, mindless bombing is surely one of the responses their grisly strategy hopes to elicit. Moreover, a major crisis in the Middle East will inescapably cause a rise in global oil prices, with, from the assassins' point of view, desirable destabilizing effects on all the economies of the advanced industrial nations.

What America should do

What should we do? The following is a start on what, in a better world, we might modestly think about doing. But let me concede at the outset that none of this is going to happen. The people in Washington who run our government believe that they can now get all the things they wanted before the trade towers came down: more money for the military, ballistic missile defenses, more freedom for the intelligence services and removal of the last modest restrictions (no assassinations, less domestic snooping, fewer lists given to "friendly" foreign police of people we want executed) that the Vietnam era placed on our leaders. An inevitable consequence of big "blowback" events like this one is that, the causes having been largely kept from American eyes (if not Islamic or Latin American ones), people cannot make the necessary connections for an explanation. Popular support for Washington is thus, at least for a while, staggeringly high.

Nonetheless, what we *should* do is to make a serious analytical effort to determine what overseas military commitments make sense and where we should pull in our horns. Although we intend to continue supporting Israel, our new policy should be to urge the dismantling of West Bank Israeli settlements as fast as possible. In Saudi Arabia, we should withdraw our troops, since they do nothing for our oil security, which we can maintain by other means. Beyond the Middle East, in Okinawa, where we have thirty-eight US military bases in the midst of 1.3 million civilians, we should start by bringing home the Third Marine Division and demobilizing it. It is understrength, has no armor and is not up to the standards of the domestically based First and Second Marine Divisions. It has no deterrent value but is, without question, an unwanted burden we force the people of this unlucky island to bear.

A particular obscenity crying out for elimination is the US Army's School of the Americas, founded in Panama in 1946 and moved to Fort Benning, Georgia, in 1984 after Panamanian President Jorge Illueca called it "the biggest base for destabilization in Latin America" and evicted it. Its curriculum includes counterinsurgency, military intelligence, interrogation techniques, sniper fire, infantry and commando tactics, psychological warfare and jungle operations. Although a few members of Congress have long tried to shut it down, the Pentagon and the White House have always found ways to keep it in the budget. In May 2000 the Clinton Administration sought to provide new camouflage for the school by renaming it the "Defense Institute for Hemispheric Security Cooperation" and transferring authority over it from the Army Department to the Defense Department.

The school has trained more than 60,000 military and police officers from Latin American and Caribbean countries. Among SOA's most illustrious graduates are the dictators Manuel Noriega (now serving a forty-year sentence in an American jail for drug trafficking) and Omar Torrijos of Panama; Guillermo Rodrigues of Ecuador; Juan Velasco Alvarado of Peru; Leopoldo Galtieri, former head of Argentina's junta; and Hugo Banzer Suarez of Bolivia. More recently, Peru's Vladimiro Montesinos, SOA class of 1965, surfaced as a CIA asset and former President Alberto Fujimori's closest adviser.

More difficult than these fairly simple reforms would be to bring our rampant militarism under control. From George Washington's "farewell address" to Dwight Eisenhower's invention of the phrase "military-industrial complex," American leaders have warned about the dangers of a bloated, permanent, expensive military establishment that has lost its relationship to the country because service in it is no longer an obligation of citizenship. Our military operates the biggest arms sales operation on earth; it rapes girls, women and schoolchildren in Okinawa; it cuts ski-lift cables in Italy, killing twenty vacationers, and dismisses what its insubordinate pilots have done as a "training accident"; it allows its nuclear attack submarines to be used for joy rides for wealthy civilian supporters and then covers up the negligence that caused the sinking of a Japanese high school training ship; it propagandizes the nation with Hollywood films glorifying military service (*Pearl Harbor*); and it manipulates the political process to get more carrier task forces, antimissile missiles, nuclear weapons, stealth bombers and other expensive gadgets for which we have no conceivable use. Two of the most influential federal institutions are not in Washington but on the south side of the Potomac River—the Defense Department and the Central Intelligence Agency. Given their influence today, one must conclude that the government outlined in the Constitution of 1787 no longer bears much relationship to the government that actually rules from Washington. Until that is corrected, we should probably stop talking about "democracy" and "human rights."

In Saudi Arabia, we should withdraw our troops, since they do nothing for our oil security.

Once we have done the analysis, brought home most of our "forward deployed" troops, refurbished our diplomatic capabilities, reassured the world that we are not unilateralists who walk away from treaty commitments and reintroduced into government the kinds of idealistic policies we once pioneered (e.g., the Marshall Plan), then we might assess what we can do against "terrorism." We could reduce our transportation and information vulnerabilities by building into our systems more of what engineers call redundancy: different ways of doing the same things—airlines and railroads, wireless and optical fiber communications, automatic computer backup programs, land routes around bridges. It is absurd that our railroads do not even begin to compare with those in Western Europe or

Japan, and their inadequacies have made us overly dependent on aviation in travel between US cities. It may well be that some public utilities should be nationalized, just as safety aboard airliners should become a federal function. Flight decks need to be made genuinely inaccessible from the passenger compartments, as they are on El Al. In what might seem a radical change, we could even hire intelligence analysts at the CIA who can read the languages of the countries they are assigned to and have actually visited the places they write about (neither of these conditions is even slightly usual at the present time).

If we do these things, the crisis will recede. If we play into the hands of the terrorists, we will see more collateral damage among our own citizens. Ten years ago, the other so-called superpower, the former Soviet Union, disappeared almost overnight because of internal contradictions, imperial overstretch and an inability to reform. We have always been richer, so it might well take longer for similar contradictions to afflict our society. But it is nowhere written that the United States, in its guise as an empire dominating the world, must go on forever.

9

The Financial Backing of Terrorist Groups Must Be Targeted

Jim Hoagland

Jim Hoagland is a Pulitzer Prize–winning columnist for the Washington Post.

A key to the war against the terrorist organizations behind the September 11 attacks is to go after their money supply. International banks and financial institutions must crack down on money laundering practices that terrorists can exploit for their benefit. In addition, the United States should act against Islamic charities that may have supported terrorist groups.

Money sets Osama bin Laden apart from other Middle Eastern fanatics and murderers. A fortune derived from Saudi Arabia's vast oil revenues buys his organization survival and "success."

Finding and destroying the money trails to bin Laden is essential to finding and destroying his group. The Bush administration must penetrate and take apart the nexus of terror that surrounds bin Laden and his Afghan and Arab allies. The nexus is geographical, ideological and religious as well as financial. But without the money, the rest would not be enough to enable these mass murderers to hatch and conceal their plots for years and then spring them on a sunny Tuesday morning of their choosing.

That agents suspected of working for this son of a Saudi billionaire struck at the World Trade Center and brought down a visible symbol of international capitalism was certainly no accident. Revenge against easy money, money that has undermined the traditional way of life in the Arabian peninsula, had a place along with revenge against America on the terrorists' twisted agenda.

It is enough to make you think that Lenin got the general idea right but the details wrong. The first Soviet leader predicted that the merchants of America and Britain would gladly sell communists the rope with which to hang the world's capitalists. But the West's symbolic weak link turns out to be oil—and the floods of money it has poured on economically primitive lands—not rope.

Finding and destroying the money trails to bin Laden is essential to finding and destroying his group.

It was jet fuel that caused the Trade Center's twin towers to burn and implode on Sept. 11. And it was oil money that enabled bin Laden to buy sanctuary first in Sudan and then Afghanistan, to assemble a small army to protect him and to field well-equipped and trained agents around the world.

Freezing assets

The White House fired a modest first shot at bin Laden's enablers last week [September 24, 2001] by freezing the U.S. assets of individuals and organizations with financial links to him. Probably more important, the Treasury Department turned on a dime from fighting significant international cooperation on dirty money havens to threatening retribution against foreign banks that did not follow the U.S. lead on bin Laden.

The Bank of International Settlements is now said to be coordinating a daily listing of suspect institutions and persons operating in the world's 10 richest countries and encouraging banking centers to sort for transactions involving them.

The U.S. list included Islamic foundations, such as the Al Rashid Trust of Pakistan and the Wafa Humanitarian Organization of Saudi Arabia. They are only the tip of an iceberg of other Islamic charity fronts that wittingly and unwittingly provide cover for bin Laden's activities in desolate, starving places such as Afghanistan and Yemen.

International banks

But going after the regional fronts is only part of the financial task. This crisis offers Washington the need and the opportunity to force American and international banks to clean up money concealment and laundering practices they now tolerate or encourage, and which terrorism can exploit.

"It is a major security problem to have the huge amount of money we know is being hidden in this system and not know who controls it," says Robert Morgenthau, New York's district attorney and a man who has thought deeply and consistently over the years about the damage the international banking system inflicts on capitalism in the pursuit of short-term profit.

In the past three years [1998–2001], bank deposits in the tiny and unregulated Cayman Islands have grown from $500 billion to $800 billion, says Morgenthau, who notes that "47 of the world's largest banks are licensed to operate" in a setting where banks are used to hide assets, launder proceeds of crimes and pay out bribes to foreign officials.

Morgenthau has tenaciously pursued difficult and time-consuming investigations into banking crimes that other prosecutors have avoided. He has found "terrorist accounts" offshore in the past—and also found little interest in Washington in pressing the banking industry to curb the secrecy and excesses that enable those accounts to be established.

"Congress is putting $40 billion into the national recovery effort," Morgenthau says. "They could recover that and more by preventing these tax havens and banks from hiding assets. We have to do our part to make taxpayers see the system is fair."

The Bush administration has put a toe into the offshore water where banks help bad guys manipulate them for evil and for mutual profit. The feds should wade in vigorously and prepare for a long struggle against all the enablers, even those in bankers' pinstripes.

10

The United States Should Seek Alternatives to Military Action

Joyce Neu

Joyce Neu is executive director of the Joan B. Kroc Institute for Peace and Justice at the University of San Diego.

Americans are justifiably angry at the terrorists behind the September 11 attacks. Many call for military reprisals. However, war has failed to deter terrorism and inevitably kills innocent bystanders and civilians. The United States should reject calls for war and revenge and instead seek out alternative ways of bringing the terrorists to justice and work to remove the underlying causes of terrorism. By responding with restraint and magnanimity, America can help prevent terrorism in the future.

In the last decade, I have seen firsthand the consequences of armed conflict in Bosnia, Congo, Georgia, Rwanda, Sudan and Uganda. As a professional in the field of conflict resolution, I have met with government and rebel leaders who argued eloquently, in the words of Bob Dylan's famous sixties song, that "God was on their side."

While each conflict may be different in its history and causes, each conflict is the same in causing the deaths of innocents. Of the several million people who have been killed in wars in the last decade, estimates are that 80 percent to 90 percent of these are civilians. No matter how just the cause, these people did not deserve to die.

As a result of the tragic events of Sept. 11, our government is examining possible responses, including military action. Polls show that most Americans favor military action; but there are those of us who believe the United States is capable of being held to a higher standard. If we believe, like the terrorists who struck the World Trade Center, the Pentagon, and a field in Pennsylvania, that our cause is just, and that innocent lives may have to be lost to extract "justice," then we become moral cowards, defining justice in terms of retribution and revenge and we perpetuate a cycle

From "Extracting Vengeance or Building a Lasting Peace," by Joyce Neu, *San Diego Union-Tribune*, September 27, 2001. Copyright © 2001 by Union-Tribune Publishing Company. Reprinted by permission of the author.

of violence all too familiar to those who perpetrated the brutal actions of Sept. 11.

The tragic loss of life of Sept. 11 has torn the mask of civility off many of our faces. We are justifiably angry and frustrated at our inability to have predicted or prevented the deaths on our soil of so many good people, Americans and others from around the world.

Responding magnanimously to violence

What kind of response can we have that will demonstrate to the world that we mean business in fighting this campaign against terrorism? Rather than look to military might as our answer, we might seek more creative, sustainable ways to ensure justice is done and that the causes for such violence are extinguished. As patriotic Americans, we may want to demonstrate to the world the power of a free society by acting internationally the way we see firefighters, police officers, and volunteers acting in response to the World Trade Center destruction—with perseverance, generosity and concern.

Why would we choose to respond magnanimously instead of militarily? Would this be seen as weakness? While military power serves as a deterrent to the threat of war between nations, it clearly has not served as a deterrent to terrorism.

Children growing up in the developing world look to the developed world, particularly the United States, as a model. Will Afghan and Iraqi children, having been subjected to hunger, disease and oppression, look at the United States as a model of what they want for their country or as the enemy on whom to seek revenge? This is within our power to decide. Responding magnanimously will sow the seeds of friendship; striking their homelands will give rise to a new generation of terrorists.

Perhaps just as importantly, if we respond militarily, what does it say about us as a people? Does it say that because we have the power to destroy, we must do so? That faced with an attack against us, we have no recourse but to respond in similar fashion? Wouldn't restraint reveal our true nature better?

That our ability to develop sophisticated weaponry does not mean that we are eager to use it? We should be clear that no matter how powerful our military is, it cannot guarantee that we can go into Afghanistan or Iraq without incurring the deaths of our own troops and those of innocent civilians.

Difficult choices

We are a nation of the people and by the people, and we are facing difficult choices: do we rationalize the deaths of innocents abroad as the cost of fighting terrorism? Do we make clear to the world that we hold human life sacred only if it is American life? Or do we find ways to safeguard our lives and property in a way that honors the foundations of our society: rule of law, human rights, and the dignity of each person?

The reactions of families whose loved ones were killed or are still missing seems to be that they do not want a military action taken in the name of their loved ones. They do not see that violence will get anything but more families torn apart in grief.

Americans should demonstrate that we are not like the terrorists and do not take the lives of innocents. We need the strength of character and moral authority to pursue a campaign to eradicate the causes of terrorism. While it may involve determining those responsible, routing them out and seeing that they are brought to justice, the campaign against terrorism must seek to pull out the roots that spread the hatred, fear and desperation that give rise to suicide and destruction.

We must begin a campaign of inoculating people against despair by taking on the economic and social disparities that give rise to hopelessness and frustration, whether in our country or outside. Americans are a generous people. The TV images of the work of firefighters, police officers and volunteers in New York City make us all proud to be Americans. We need to take this selflessness to those in need in our own country as well as outside our country.

Helping others

Just as we export goods, so should we export our know-how, our decency, and our conviction that working together, we can make a difference. One part of our covert campaign against terrorism therefore should consist of rebuilding schools and hospitals, providing training and skills for responsible leadership, and in the short-term, making sure that there are refugee camps ready with food and shelter to accept people fleeing from the feared U.S. military attacks.

Another part of the campaign is to make clear the distinction between religion and fanaticism. Just as many wars are supposedly waged in the name of religion, there are usually other, more material reasons for the violence. Islam is not the enemy just as Arab countries are not the enemy. These acts were the acts of terrorists. Not Islamic terrorists, not Arab terrorists—just terrorists. Our leaders have started to make this clear and we need to continue to emphasize that these acts had nothing to do with any religion or belief system. God was not on their side just as God is not on the side of anyone who perpetrates the killing and destruction of innocent people.

Polls show that most Americans favor military action; but there are those of us who believe the United States is capable of being held to a higher standard.

The United States should also re-engage in the dialogue to establish a permanent International Criminal Court. Although discussions in the United Nations and other international arenas often take positions that the U.S. government believes are antithetical to ours, if we are not part of the debate, then we cannot complain when we do not like the outcome.

The United States has gained a reputation for walking out of difficult discussions, as we did at the U.N. Conference on Racism and Related Intolerance. We should have stronger stomachs and stay engaged. These terrorist acts are abundant evidence that if we won't deal with the problems in the world, they will come to us.

Without an International Criminal Court, we will have to create ad hoc tribunals for people like Osama bin Laden. The world deserves a permanent, standing court where terrorists and war criminals, regardless of country or conflict, can be tried.

Finally, we need to take time to mourn the dead and the missing. Before we react in a manner that undermines our character as a strong and proud people who believe in the rule of law and justice, our leaders should take the time to remember the lessons of U.S. involvement in Japan and Germany post-World War II.

By helping those countries and peoples rebuild and develop, we gained loyal allies that are still with us today. Let us create new allies out of enemies so that our children and grandchildren will remember Sept. 11, 2001 and its victims as giving rise to new understandings and tolerance, not to more violence and death.

11

The Terrorist Attacks Should Be Treated as Acts of War

Gary Dempsey

Gary Dempsey is a foreign policy analyst at the Cato Institute, a libertarian public policy think tank.

Some people have described the September 11 terrorist incidents in New York and Washington as "crimes against humanity" and have argued that the perpetrators should be captured, charged, and tried in an international court. However, treating terrorism as a criminal justice problem has failed in the past to deter terrorists or to hold foreign governments responsible for harboring or sponsoring terrorists. The terrorist assaults were acts of war against the American people. The U.S. government must respond accordingly by going to war against the perpetrators of those acts in order to protect Americans from more attacks.

A global coalition of human rights groups described the ghastly terrorist attacks on the World Trade Center and the Pentagon as "crimes against humanity." They added that the incidents proved the United States should reconsider its opposition to the creation of a standing international criminal court. Never mind that the international community has yet to agree on a legal definition of international terrorism or that a global court could open a Pandora's box of legal mischief—treating terrorism as a criminal justice matter is wrongheaded.

President Bill Clinton's responses to terrorism

Yet that is the way the Clinton administration chose to deal with the problem. Indeed, the 2000 bombing of the USS Cole (which killed 17 and wounded 33), the 1998 bombing of two U.S. embassies in east Africa (which killed 224 and wounded more than 4,000), and the 1993 bombing of the World Trade Center (which killed six and wounded more than 1,000), were all pursued as criminal justice matters. America's law enforcement agencies conducted investigations and eventually made some arrests. The result: 12 men involved in the 1993 World Trade Center bombing were convicted in November 1997, four years after their attack, and four men involved in the 1998 embassy bombings were convicted in May 2001, three years after their attack. The mastermind of the bombings, Osama bin Laden, remained at-large and was put on the FBI's 10 Most Wanted list. No one has yet been convicted for the Cole attack.

Treating terrorism as a criminal justice matter is wrongheaded.

According to a former Clinton administration official, the goal in treating international terrorism as a legal matter was to "depoliticize" and "delegitimize" it by defining it as criminal activity instead of warfare. Resorting to indictments, extraditions, and trials, it was argued, was the best course. "We are not a nation that retaliates just in order to get vengeance," exclaimed then-secretary of state Madeleine Albright after the U.S. embassy bombings. "America does not forget our own legal system while searching for those who harmed us." Such thinking continues today. University of Illinois law professor Francis Boyle, for example, says that Osama bin Laden "is a fugitive from justice and this should be handled as a matter as other fugitives from justice of international law enforcement."

But defining what happened in New York and Washington as crimes misses the point. One of the primary constitutional responsibilities of the U.S. government is to defend the American people from external attack. It's striking, then, that the last [Clinton] administration and its defenders were so willing to use the U.S. military for social work and peacekeeping around the world—mostly on missions that had little to do with the direct security of America—but treated the slaughter of American citizens and destruction of U.S. property by international terrorists as a law enforcement issue.

That approach has hardly proven a model of deterrence. It has neither held foreign governments sufficiently accountable for harboring, let alone sponsoring, terrorist organizations, nor confronted the root causes of what drives terrorists to target America in the first place.

That said, the magnitude of the attacks on New York and Washington and the perpetrators' demonstrable willingness to keep escalating their efforts (perhaps biological, chemical, or nuclear weapons next time) make it clear that countering terrorism can no longer be primarily a matter for the law enforcement or even the intelligence communities. The prospect of jail time is not a substitute for defense policy.

Acts of war

Sadly, even a radical shift in America's Middle East and Persian Gulf policies at this point is unlikely to reverse the built-up momentum of the terrorist threat. That means the United States has little choice now but to respond to the recent attacks as only the initial acts of war and to defend its citizens by taking the war back to bin Laden and whomever else supports him.

It wouldn't be the first time the United States has gone to war against non-state actors. In 1801, President Thomas Jefferson went to war against the Barbary pirates, who preyed upon European and American shipping in both Mediterranean and Atlantic waters. James Madison supported Jefferson's efforts, which proved successful by 1805.

Jefferson, unfortunately, operated without a formal declaration of war from Congress. He later admitted that he was "unauthorized by the Constitution, without the sanction of Congress, to go beyond the line of defense," and that it was the prerogative of Congress to authorize "measures of offense also." Lamentably, Congress last week [on September 14, 2001] sidestepped its duty to formally declare war and instead granted the president the authority "to use all necessary force."

Of course, formally declaring war would not mean that U.S. bombers must immediately launch air strikes or that the Marines must eventually conduct a full-scale land invasion. Rather, it would signify that a profound threshold has been crossed and that there are certain things Americans absolutely will not tolerate happening to their fellow citizens.

12

The Terrorist Attacks Should Be Treated as International Crimes

David Held

David Held is a professor of political science at the London School of Economics and author of Democracy and the Global Order *and other works.*

The terrorism of September 11 was an attack on fundamental and global principles of justice and law. The response to them must be careful and measured, and should not contradict these fundamental principles of civilization. While war and bombing are one option, another is the creation of an international commission on global terrorism under the auspices of the United Nations. Criminalizing terrorism on an international basis can foster global cooperation in capturing and bringing those responsible for the September 11 attack to justice. In addition, nations must work together to address social justice issues and underlying grievances that may contribute to the rise of terrorist groups.

The greatest Enlightenment philosopher, Immanuel Kant, wrote over two hundred years ago that we are 'unavoidably side by side'. A violent abrogation of law and justice in one place has consequences for many other places and can be experienced everywhere. While he dwelt on these matters and their implications at length, he could not have known how profound and immediate his concerns would become.

Since Kant, our mutual interconnectedness and vulnerability have grown rapidly. We no longer live, if we ever did, in a world of discrete national communities which have the power and capacity alone to determine the fate of those within them. Instead, we live in a world of overlapping communities of fate. The trajectories and futures of nation-states are now heavily enmeshed with each other. In our world, it is not only the violent exception that links people together across borders, the very nature of everyday problems and processes joins people in multiple ways.

From the movement of ideas and cultural artifacts to the fundamental issues raised by genetic engineering, from the conditions of financial stability to environmental degradation, the fate and fortunes of each of us
are thoroughly intertwined.

The story of our increasingly global order is not a singular one. There
are many myths about globalisation and one in particular is pernicious;
that is, that the age is increasingly defined by global markets, economic
processes and social forces which necessarily escape the control of states
and politicians. The spread of markets for goods, services and finance has,
indeed, altered the political terrain. But the story of globalisation is not
just one of the expansion of markets, neoliberal deregulation and the ab-
dication of politics; for it is also one of growing aspirations for international law and justice. From the UN system to the EU [European Union],
from changes to the law of war to the entrenchment of human rights,
from the emergence of international environmental regimes to the foundation of the International Criminal Court, there is also another narrative
being told—the narrative which seeks to reframe human activity and entrench it in law, rights and responsibilities.

This is why the 11th September is a defining moment for humankind. The terrorist violence was an atrocity of extraordinary proportions;
it was a crime against America and against humanity; it was an outrage
that ranks amongst the worlds most heinous crimes; and it was, make no
mistake about it, an attack on the fundamental principles of freedom,
democracy, the rule of law and justice.

Fundamental global principles

These principles are not just western principles. Elements of them had
their origins in the early modern period in the West, but their validity ex-
tends much further than this. For these principles are the basis of a fair,
humane and decent society, of whatever religion or cultural tradition. To
paraphrase the American legal theorist Bruce Ackerman, there is no nation
without a woman who yearns for equal rights, no society without a man
who denies the need for deference and no developing country without a
person who does not wish for the minimum means of subsistence so that
they may go about their everyday lives. The principles of freedom, democracy and justice are the basis for articulating and entrenching the equal liberty of all human beings, wherever they were born or brought up.

The 11th September is a defining moment for
humankind.

The intensity of the range of responses to the atrocities of 11th September is fully understandable from any perspective. There cannot be
many people in the world (despite media images of celebrations in some
quarters) who did not experience shock, revulsion, horror, disbelief, anger
and a desire for vengeance. This emotional range is perfectly natural
within the context of the immediate events. But it cannot be the basis for
a more considered and wise response.

The founding principles of our society, the very principles under attack on 11th September, dictate that we pause for reflection; that we do not overgeneralise our response from one moment and one set of events; that we do not jump to conclusions based on concerns that emerge in one particular country; and that we do not re-write and re-work history from one place.

The fight against terror must be put on a new footing. There can be no going back to the haphazard and complacent approach to terrorism of 10th September. Terrorists must be brought to heel and those who protect and nurture them must be brought to account. Zero tolerance is fully justified in these circumstances. Terrorism negates our most cherished principles and ambitions.

The fight against terror must be put on a new footing.

But any defensible, justifiable and sustainable response to the 11th September must be consistent with our founding principles and the aspirations of international society for security, law, and the impartial administration of justice—aspirations painfully articulated after the Holocaust and the Second World War. If the means deployed to fight terrorism contradict these principles, then the emotion of the moment might be satisfied, but our mutual vulnerability will be deepened. We will be set on yet another step backwards from a more secure and just world order. This could easily involve the growth of intolerance of all attempts to protest over and change political circumstances, even if they are law abiding and peaceful in their orientations.

Another option

War and bombing are one option for the immediate future; but another is an International Commission on global terrorism which might be modelled on the Nuremberg and Tokyo war tribunals, working under the authority of a reenergised and revitalised United Nations. Such a commission could be empowered to investigate those responsible for the new mass terrorism and to bring them to justice. Backed by the capacity to impose economic, political and military sanctions—and supported by UN and NATO military capacities, among others—it might be the basis of an investigation and system of punishment which commands global support. It could be the basis not only for the strengthening of existing legal and multilateral arrangements, but the basis for helping to define a new just, accountable and democratic order. The means would be consistent with the defence of the principles under threat. Terrorism must be criminalised on an international basis, not eradicated through arbitrary violent action.

I am not a pacifist. The motivation for these recommendations is not the avoidance of the use of coercive force under all circumstances. Rather, it is anchored on the wish to build on the more humane and just elements of our global order which have been set down in the last several decades, and to entrench them in such a way that could command the respect and loyalty of all peoples, everywhere.

But to borrow a phrase, we must be tough not just on crime but on the causes of crime. Whoever the perpetrators were of the terrorism of 11th September, we know that there will always be volunteers for suicide missions, suicide bombings, and for terrorist groupings if we do not concern ourselves with the wider issues of peace and social justice in the global community. In our global age shaped by the flickering images of television and new information systems, the gross inequalities of life chances found in many of the world's regions feed a frenzy of anger, hostility and resentment. Without a just peace in the Middle East and without an attempt to anchor globalisation in meaningful principles of social justice, there can be no durable solution to the kind of crimes we have just seen.

Of course, such crimes may often be the work of the simply deranged and the fanatic and so there can be no guarantee that a more just world will be a more peaceful one in all respects. But if we turn our back on these challenges altogether, there is no hope of ameliorating the social basis of disadvantage often experienced in the poorest and most dislocated countries. Gross injustices, linked to a sense of hopelessness born of generations of neglect, feed anger and hostility. Popular support against terrorism depends upon convincing people that there is a legal and pacific way of addressing their grievances.

Kant was right; the violent abrogation of law and justice in one place ricochets across the world. We cannot accept the burden of putting justice right in one dimension of life—security—without at the same time seeking to put it right everywhere.

13

Bombing Afghanistan Is the Wrong Response to the Terrorist Attacks

Matthew Rothschild

Matthew Rothschild is editor of the Progressive, *a monthly magazine that champions peace and social justice.*

President George W. Bush's October 7, 2001, decision to bomb Afghanistan was a risky and unjustified move. The people of Afghanistan were not responsible for the September 11 terrorist attacks and should not be killed by American bombs. Bush is embarking on a doomed crusade that will likely create as many terrorists as it destroys. The United States should instead get at the root causes of terrorism, including Third World poverty and repression.

B y bombing Afghanistan, George W. Bush has rolled the bombs as if they were dice. And for all his protestations to the contrary, he has treated the people of Afghanistan as if they were playthings.

When the United States and Britain bombed Kabul, a city of more than two million people, and at least three other cities—Kandahar, Herat, and Jalalabad—they guaranteed that innocent Afghans would lose their lives. These Afghans did not fly planes into the World Trade towers or the Pentagon. They did nothing to deserve death at the hands of Washington.

How many innocent Afghans ultimately die in this war we will not know.

But what we do know is that Bush calculated that their deaths were worth it.

They are not.

Killing innocent people is never justified.

Making America less safe

And this war will not make the United States any safer; it will make this country more imperiled.

Already, the government is warning us of additional, and perhaps imminent, terrorist attacks on our soil.

Already, the government is nervous that Pakistan may fall to forces allied with the Taliban, and that Pakistan's nuclear weapons may not be secure.

Already, there is great anxiety in Washington about the negative response this war will spark in the rest of the Muslim world.

War is a terribly risky and dangerous game. But Bush was eager to play it.

Like his father in the Gulf War, George W. spurned a last minute offer to negotiate. The Taliban offered to release the eight Americans under arrest and apprehend Osama bin Laden and try him under Islamic law; the United States didn't give it a second thought.

Bush has vowed to wage an unlimited war. "You will have every tool you need," he assured his soldiers on Sunday [October 7, 2001], echoing his words of September 20, when he said the United States would use "every necessary weapon of war."

Does that include nuclear weapons?

The war is also unlimited in time and in location.

It was not reassuring to hear Bush say on Sunday that this war in Afghanistan was just "phase one."

How many phases does he have in mind?

This war will not make the United States any safer; it will make this country more imperiled.

"Today, we focus on Afghanistan, but the battle is broader," he said. "Every nation has a choice to make. In this conflict, there is no neutral ground. If any government sponsors the outlaws and killers of innocents, they have become outlaws and murderers themselves. And they will take that lonely path at their own peril."

Wait a second here.

Congress did not grant Bush the title of grand executioner of global terrorism.

As vast as the Congressional resolution authorizing the use of force was, it was limited to the culprits behind the September 11 attack.

But Bush is not content to stop there. He sees himself on a zealous mission, and he is unilaterally and illegally grabbing power to undertake it.

The most powerful man in the world, unchecked by Congress and the media, now suffers delusions of military grandeur, and innocent people will pay with their lives.

A doomed mission

It's a mission that is doomed from the start.

He cannot kill every terrorist in the world.

(And by the way, is he going to bomb Bogotá because it works with the paramilitaries, who are "outlaws and killers of innocents"? Unlikely, since Colombia is our ally in the war on drugs.)

What's more, the bombings are probably already creating more terrorists at this very moment, who will be willing to kill and die to stand up to an America they see as the aggressor.

Yes, Osama bin Laden and Al Qaeda, or whoever were the authors of the atrocity of September 11, need to be brought to justice. They should be apprehended and hauled before an international tribunal for committing a crime against humanity.

And yes, the United States needs to secure itself against future attacks.

But terrorism itself will not disappear after bin Laden and Al Qaeda are gone.

It will not disappear if Bush levels Kabul, Baghdad, Khartoum, and Damascus, all at once, as some on the far reaches of the Republican Party seem to be proposing.

Roots of terror

War is not the answer. The answer is getting at the roots of terror.

And there are many roots, some of them watered by the United States.

It watered them in Afghanistan in the 1980s by recruiting, arming, and training tens of thousands of Islamic fundamentalists and by virtually reviving the very concept of jihad.

It watered them during the Gulf War and especially afterwards, when the United States insisted that the U.N. impose economic sanctions that have killed more than 500,000 Iraqi children.

It watered them for the last thirty-four years by backing Israel even as it maintained its illegal occupation of Palestinian land and repressed Palestinians on a daily basis.

Some roots are separate, watered by one of the longest polluted rivers in the world, which is anti-Semitism, or watered by another rancid pool, which is religious fundamentalism.

Add to that the combination of Third World poverty and repressive rule (both of which the United States bears some responsibility for), and you can get a handle on the complex phenomenon that is terrorism.

These roots cannot be eradicated at gunpoint; they cannot be pulled up by bombs.

But many of them can be dried up if the United States adopted a more benign foreign policy. (And it certainly would help if Bush spoke in a secular, not a religious, voice. There he was again Sunday telling us all about his prayers.)

Bush has set the nation upon an endless course of war.

For the moment, the people are behind him.

But this might change.

The costs of war may soon be excessive: in innocent lives killed abroad; in the deaths of U.S. soldiers; in a wobbly and swooning economy; in world chaos.

Bush has rolled the bombs. Now we all may feel the fallout.

14

Bombing Afghanistan Was a Necessary Step in the War Against Terrorism

Michael Kelly

Michael Kelly is the editor of the Atlantic Monthly *and a columnist for the* Washington Post. *He is the author of* Martyrs' Day: Chronicle of a Small War, *an account of his experiences as a journalist covering the 1991 Persian Gulf War.*

The bombing of Afghanistan that began on October 7, 2001, was America's answer to the September 11 terrorist attacks. Those who still question whether it was the right answer should pay close attention to terrorist leader Osama bin Laden's taped message released that day, in which he calls for Muslims to engage in holy war against America and the West. The terrorists led by bin Laden constitute a serious threat to Americans, who should be prepared for a long, daunting, but necessary war.

Sunday [October 7, 2001] was a day of clarification on various levels. The first was the most basic. We have been under attack by Osama bin Laden and his al Qaeda network for some years now, but we did not fully admit to that until Sept. 11. On Oct. 7 we answered Sept. 11. There was a feeling to the day of something like relief. Well, that's that; war is joined, and we must win it.

What we must win was also made clear. Incredibly, in the light of 6,000 dead, some (mostly on the left) have persisted in the delusion that we are involved here in something that can be put into some sort of context of normality—a crisis that can be resolved through legal or diplomatic efforts, or handled with United Nations resolutions, or addressed by limited military "reprisals." We have been warned not to see this in too-large terms—as a holy war, or a crusade or a clash of civilizations.

Osama bin Laden himself put the lie to all that with a videotaped message that apparently had been recorded after Sept. 11 but in anticipation of Oct. 7. In this statement, released to the Al-Jazeera television network, bin Laden abandoned the shred of pretense that he was not responsible for the attacks of Sept. 11. He crowed his joy: "Here is America struck by God Almighty in one of its vital organs, so that its greatest buildings are destroyed. Grace and gratitude to God. America has been filled with horror from North to South and East to West, and thanks be to God."

He described the conflict repeatedly in the terms of holy war. "These events have divided the world into two camps, the camp of the faithful and the camp of infidels," he said. And: "Every Muslim must rise to defend his religion." He ended with a promise: "I swear to God that America will not live in peace before peace reigns in Palestine, and before all the army of infidels depart the land of Mohammed, peace be upon him."

Is that clear now?

President Bush's resolve

The way in which our government views this war was also made clear. In his address to the nation on Sunday, Bush dropped any suggestion that what we are about is merely a manhunt on a massive scale. He made plain that America is, in fact, at war not only with bin Laden's al Qaeda but also with the Taliban forces of Afghanistan. Bush used language—"sustained, comprehensive and relentless operations"—intended to signal that, while this may be an unconventional war, it will be a war in full, not a Clintonian exercise in a spot of bombing, a bit of missile-rattling. He went further even, warning in hard language that the war could spread to other nations that sponsor terror against America: "If any government sponsors the outlaws and killers of innocents, they have become outlaws and murderers themselves. And they will take that lonely path at their own peril."

So there it is, out on the table. We are in a war, and we will be in it for some time, and this war is being undertaken toward a great and daunting end. With Sunday's speech, no one can doubt that President Bush and his advisers see the war on the same scale of magnitude as bin Laden sees it. It is us against them, and "them" has been defined broadly enough to encompass any state that harbors or sponsors anti-American terrorism. The goal here is not to knock off a few of terrorism's foot soldiers. It is to put out of business terrorism's masters, its networks and its protectors—even if those protectors enjoy status as sovereign regimes.

That this is a goal worth fighting for may be judged by the extraordinary international support for the American effort. The world's leaders know, as Britain's Tony Blair said Sunday, that the atrocity of Sept. 11 was "an attack on us all," by fanatics who threaten "any nation throughout the world that does not share their fanatical views."

No one can know how what began on Sunday will proceed. It is certainly possible that it will proceed badly, at least at times. It may appear, at times, that it will end badly. But we start out with a serious and large intent, facing an enemy that is likewise serious and likewise ambitious. If we remember this, if we stay serious and remember that the enemy too is serious, we will win. And it should not be hard to remember this. We have 6,000 reasons to never forget.

15

The Attacks Revealed America's Lack of Preparedness Against Terrorism

Franklin Foer

Franklin Foer is an associate editor of the New Republic, *a weekly journal of political analysis and opinion.*

Many of the actions the U.S. government has taken following the September 11, 2001, attacks had been previously recommended by various blue-ribbon commissions on terrorism. One of the most publicized and prescient reports on terrorism was issued in 2000 by the National Commission on Terrorism (NCT). The NCT was commissioned by Congress to analyze American counter-terrorism policy. However, its recommendations on reducing U.S. vulnerabilities to terrorist attacks were not enacted, in part because of opposition of civil liberties groups and in part because of resistance by government agencies that opposed changes in their powers and operations. America's lack of preparedness may be partially responsible for the events of September 11.

Two weeks after George W. Bush's [September 2001] declaration of war against terrorism, a battle plan is taking shape. We are putting the screws to Pakistan to end its history of mentoring terrorists. We will now treat Afghanistan like the rogue state that it is. The Treasury Department will try to choke off Osama bin Laden's financing. Intelligence agencies, at long last, will share information with one another. And if the Bush administration has its way, the CIA will revert to its pre-1995 guidelines, which allowed operatives to recruit informants with sketchy human rights records.

All sensible moves. And they were just as sensible when the National Commission on Terrorism proposed them more than a year [before the attack]. Yet the NCT's proposals never made it into law, and the reasons why say a lot about how difficult it will be for George W. Bush to carry out his war on terrorism today. The commission, you see, wasn't merely undermined by civil liberties groups suspicious of a serious effort against terrorism. It was undone by the very government agencies tasked with carrying out that effort.

A prominent commission

In Washington, blue-ribbon anti-terrorism commissions aren't exactly rare. But from the beginning, the NCT stood out. For starters, there was its mandate: It was commissioned by Congress, in the wake of the 1998 African embassy bombings, to produce the definitive blueprint for legislation overhauling counterterrorism policy. Then there was the panel's prestige. Chaired by Ronald Reagan's counterterrorism czar, L. Paul Bremer III, the commission included a retired head of the Army's Special Operations Command (Wayne Downing), a former undersecretary of defense (Fred Iklé), and a cast of foreign policy heavyweights. So unlike many other commissions whose reports get a paragraph on A-23, the NCT grabbed the attention of editorialists and Sunday talk show hosts. As former CIA director R. James Woolsey, another of the NCT panelists, puts it, "This was the best shot at change."

And the report lived up to its billing. Even its cover—which includes an image of the World Trade Center towers—was prescient. The panel found that the U.S. government wasn't prepared to prevent an Al Qaeda attack on American soil and that "the threat of attacks creating massive casualties is growing." In response, the NCT called for, among other things, expanded wiretap authority, recruitment of linguists, and the revision of laws that prevent the FBI and CIA from sharing intelligence—exactly what John Ashcroft is calling for now.

Opposition to NCT recommendations

Civil liberties groups were predictably hostile. Within hours of the report's release, the American Civil Liberties Union (ACLU) called it an "ominous cloud." The Arab American Institute's James Zogby said it harked back to the "darkest days of the McCarthy era." Leftist commentators accused the commission of hyping the danger of terrorism so that the FBI and CIA could justify greater surveillance powers and more money. *Salon*'s Bruce Shapiro suggested that the NCT's warnings of domestic attack "are a con job, with roughly the veracity of the latest Robert Ludlum novel." Robert Dreyfuss wrote in *Mother Jones* that "[f]or the national security establishment, adrift with few enemies since the end of the Cold War a decade ago, the terrorist threat seems made to order."

But the national security establishment objected to the commission's recommendations as well. Testifying before Congress in 1999, FBI director Louis Freeh tried to anticipate the report's complaints, noting that "[t]he frequency of terrorist incidents in the United States has decreased in number" and implying that the bureau was already effectively combating the danger. The CIA was even more hostile. When the report appeared, CIA spokesman Bill Harlow rejected its call for the agency to jettison its "overly risk averse" approach to recruiting informants. Three members of the commission told me that the CIA leaked the report's more controversial recommendations in order to put the NCT on the defensive.

In part, the CIA opposed the recommendations out of fear that they would rekindle the agency's cold war reputation for dirty tricks. Under Bill Clinton, the CIA furiously tried to scrub away the tarnish of its Latin American misadventures during the 1980s, especially its alliance with Guatemalan paramilitary squads. And the NCT seemed to be pushing in the opposite direction, explicitly pleading with the CIA to find more "unsavory" terrorist sources. "Since John Deutch headed the agency," one ex-CIA official told me, "the seventh floor of Langley has become very politically correct. And they're so worried about provoking critics."

The NCT's proposals never made it into law, and the reasons why say a lot about how difficult it will be . . . to carry out . . . [a] war on terrorism today.

But mostly, the CIA opposed the NCT's recommendations for the same reason virtually every other government department and agency did: They trespassed on its turf. On CNN's *Late Edition*, Madeleine Albright countered the NCT's finding that the administration needed to get tougher with Pakistan and Greece. "We are pressing them [already]," she told Wolf Blitzer. And she warned that "in looking at how we fight [terrorism], we have to remember what kind of a society we are"—implying that the commission wanted to trample civil liberties. Deputy Attorney General Eric Holder told reporters that the NCT recommendations siphoned too much power away from the FBI. And the administration's civil rights chief, Bill Lan Lee, implied in a speech to the American-Arab Anti-Discrimination Committee that Arab-Americans were being unfairly smeared. (Never mind that the report didn't once mention Arab-Americans.)

A missed opportunity

Still, for one brief moment, Congress looked like it might impose change. Using the NCT report as their template, in July 2000 Senators Jon Kyl and Dianne Feinstein attached the recommended reforms to an intelligence authorization bill. As one Senate staffer told me, "It could have been one of the most important overhauls of American intelligence in recent memory." But the Kyl-Feinstein legislation quickly ran aground thanks largely to one man: Vermont's Patrick Leahy. Warning of CIA mischief and "risks to important civil liberties we hold dear," Leahy threatened to hold up the entire intelligence authorization bill to sink the reforms; so Kyl and Feinstein untethered the proposals from the budgetary process. Then, in October, bin Laden blew a hole in the USS *Cole* and Kyl and Feinstein's effort gained new momentum. But this time, instead of trying to defeat the legislation outright, Leahy weakened it so much that it became essentially useless. By threatening to place a hold on the bill, he extracted countless concessions. And when the legislation finally cleared the Senate in November, it did nothing to loosen CIA recruitment guidelines or expand the FBI's wiretapping authority. "It was so watered down by the time we got the bill," says one House Republican aide, "it wasn't worth taking up." And so the legislation died.

Would the Kyl-Feinstein changes have prevented September 11? Who knows? But September 11 utterly confirmed the commission's assertion that the government agencies charged with fighting terrorism were doing a woefully inadequate job. Unfortunately, those agencies proved more skilled at protecting themselves from bureaucratic encroachment than at protecting the country from Al Qaeda. And they received critical help from civil libertarians who saw counterterrorism as merely a ruse for the expansion of government power. In Washington, denial was a river in Egypt. And barely anyone except the NCT believed that terrorists might be lurking on its banks.

16

The Terrorist Attacks Clarified the Meaning of Good and Evil

William J. Bennett

William J. Bennett, a former secretary of education, is a director of Empower America, a public policy organization, and the author of several books, including The Book of Virtues.

The terrible terrorist attacks of September 11, 2001, have brought a sense of moral clarity to the United States. For too long teachers and other influential leaders have questioned whether good and evil really exist, or whether America is truly better than its enemies. Such questioning should be a thing of the past in the wake of September 11.

In the aftermath of the attacks on the World Trade Center and the Pentagon, America will be changed politically, militarily, culturally, psychologically. It is too close to the events to understand their full impact. But one certain result is that these events have forced us to clarify and answer again universal questions that have been muddled over the past four decades.

Speaking about World War II, C.S. Lewis put it this way: "The war creates no absolutely new situation. It simply aggravates the permanent human situation so that we can no longer ignore it. Human life has always been lived on the edge of a precipice."

A moment of moral clarity

For too long, we have ignored the hostility shown toward America and democratic principles by some Muslims who adhere to a militant and radical interpretation of the Koran. We have created a moral equivalence between Israel and the Palestinians who seek to eradicate Israel. We have ignored Islamic clarion calls for our destruction and the bombings of our embassies and the U.S. destroyer Cole. This situation has not changed,

From "Faced with Evil on a Grand Scale, Nothing Is Relative," by William J. Bennett, *Los Angeles Times*, October 1, 2001. Copyright © 2001 by the *Los Angeles Times*. Reprinted with permission.

62

but now we realize what the situation is. This is a moment of moral clarity in the United States. For almost 40 years, we have been a nation that has questioned whether good and evil, right and wrong, true and false really exist. Some—particularly those in our institutions of higher learning and even some inside our own government—have wondered whether America is really better than its enemies around the world. After the events of Sept. 11, we should no longer be unsure of these things, even in the academy. We have seen the face and felt the hand of evil. Moral clarity should bring with it moral confidence and we must be reassured of some things.

America was not punished because we are bad, but because we are good.

Good and evil have never gone away; we merely had the luxury to question their existence. At the beginning of Allan Bloom's classic *The Closing of the American Mind*, he says, "There is one thing a professor can be absolutely certain of: Almost every student entering the university believes, or says he believes, that truth is relative." Can one culture, it was asked, really presume to say what should be the case in other cultures? Are there any cross-cultural values?

Yes. The use of commercial airplanes as missiles, guided into buildings where civilians work, is evil. The goal of the hijackers was the intentional destruction of innocent life so as to strike fear into the heart of America. And what they did was wrong. Not wrong given our point of view or because we were the victims or because of our Judeo-Christian tradition but simply wrong.

It has been said that these attacks were the inevitable reaction to modern-day American imperialism. They are retribution, it is claimed, for our support of Israel, our attacks on Saddam Hussein, cruise missiles launched at Afghanistan and Sudan.

Americans are good

This is nonsense. America's support for human rights and democracy is our noblest export to the world. And when we act in accord with those principles, time after time after time, we act well and honorably. We are not hated because we support Israel; we are hated because liberal democracy is incompatible with militant Islam. Despite what Hussein and Osama bin Laden and, shamefully, some American clerics have said, America was not punished because we are bad, but because we are good.

It is, therefore, past time for what novelist Tom Wolfe has called the "great relearning." We have engaged in a frivolous dalliance with dangerous theories—relativism, historicism, values clarification. Now, when faced with evil on such a grand scale, we should see these theories for what they are: empty. We must begin to have the courage of our convictions, to believe that some actions are good and some evil and to act on those beliefs to prevent evil.

And so we must respond to these attacks and prevent future attacks.

We do this to protect our own citizens and our own way of life. We do this to protect the idea that good and evil exist and that man is capable of soaring to great heights and sinking to terrible lows. We do this, in the end, to prevent the world from becoming the prisoner of terrorists, their way of battle, their way of thinking, their way of life, their way of death.

The recognition that some things are right and some things are wrong has come at a terrible cost of thousands of lives lost. The only comparable tragedy in American history, I believe, was the Civil War. And so we must join in the hopes of our 16th president and pray "that these dead shall not have died in vain, that this nation under God shall have a new birth of freedom and that government of the people, by the people, for the people shall not perish from the Earth."

17

Evil Is Too Simplistic an Explanation for the Terrorist Attacks

Joel Bleifuss

Joel Bleifuss is editor of In These Times, *a newsmagazine that promotes political and economic democracy.*

While the killing of thousands of innocents understandably gives rise to feelings of anger and hate, defining the subsequent struggle as a "monumental struggle of good versus evil," as President George W. Bush has done, oversimplifies the tragedy and brings Americans down to the level of the terrorists. Too often in history, mass atrocities have been committed against people and groups demonized as the evil enemy. Americans should resist such thinking.

The slaughter of thousands of innocent people in the attacks on the World Trade Center and the Pentagon gives rise to sharp emotions—numbness, sorrow, horror, despair, fear, anger, revenge and hate. All these feelings are understandable. Not all are noble.

In the wake of this atrocity, President George W. Bush is talking war. He defined the enemy stalking our world as an "evil" force. He characterized this war as "a monumental struggle of good versus evil."

Rallying the nation against dark forces may accomplish the administration's political objectives—putting a white hat on Bush while priming public opinion for the counterattack, and death of more innocent people, that is sure to follow. But pandering to people's fear of evil does nothing to promote peace. Indeed, it stokes the worst in human nature.

In Chicago after the attacks, a Muslim grade school was attacked with a Molotov cocktail; "Kill the Arabs" graffiti was scrawled along a major thoroughfare; more than 300 people waving American flags marched on a mosque in suburban Bridgeview.

From "The Problem with Evil," by Joel Bleifuss, *In These Times*, October 15, 2001. Copyright © 2001 by the Institute for Public Affairs. Reprinted with permission.

A simplistic explanation

Yes, people throughout history have done immensely cruel things to their fellow human beings. In some cases, the perpetrators are innately bad seeds—evil, if you will. Yet that is all too simple.

Eighteenth-century Americans and English gave smallpox-infected blankets to the Indians. Southern plantation owners traded captive African slaves like animals. Upstanding citizens persecuted German-Americans in World War I and Japanese-Americans in World War II. Members of the U.S. military bombed the people of Vietnam back to the Stone Age. This is not to mention the ongoing imposition by some Western leaders of sanctions against Iraq that have cost perhaps a million lives.

Were these historical actors all evil? Or were they, more often than not, normal folks who employed rationalizations to deny the humanity of people who were different, who were "the enemy," or who were conveniently deemed less than human to bolster the power of the established order?

One can also play the game of comparing crimes. The day after the bombings, the *New York Times'* Clyde Haberman took the your-atrocity-is-bigger-than-mine approach. He used the attacks on New York and Washington to justify Israel's policy of targeted killings, asking "Do you get it now?" to those who "damned Israel for taking admittedly harsh measures to keep its citizens alive."

In a similar vein, other commentators, mostly on the left, have explained, in some ways excused, the attacks as the understandable reaction of people subjugated to years of persecution.

All of these relativist justifications are problematic. They deny the power of human agency and thereby excuse the inexcusable—attacks on the World Trade Center and the Pentagon by Islamic extremists or Israel's state-sponsored assassinations. An action (or reaction) may be understandable—we do get it—but that doesn't make it right.

Need for leadership

It is no help at all for Bush to simplify the situation as a battle between good and evil. Such a stance, though publicly palatable, reduces things to such a degree that all subtlety and complexity is gone.

As Gary Younge observed in the *Guardian* of London: "Right now America needs a statesman, but wants a cowboy. Bush must steel himself to lead, not allow himself to follow."

Alas, this president, apparently incapable of speaking on his own, is not up to the task. When Bush, puppet-like, repeatedly invokes the word "evil," his peaceful intentions, indeed his competence, must be questioned.

Too often in modern history the inhuman "enemy" has been deemed "evil" as a prelude to mass death. Such was the thinking, no doubt, that went through the heads of the men who plotted the carnage visited on New York and Washington. But for our elected leaders to respond with the same kind of mindset can only make this tragic situation worse.

18

The World Must Respond to the Attack on New York City

Rudolph W. Giuliani

At the time of the September 11, 2001, attacks, Rudolph W. Giuliani was finishing a second term as mayor of New York City. He addressed the United Nations General Assembly at a special session on terrorism on October 1, 2001.

New York City, the most diverse city in the world, was the victim of a vicious and unjustified attack. The terrorist attacks were directed at the ideals of the United States and the United Nations, including peace, tolerance, and political and economic freedom. While the long-term solution to terrorism is the spread of the principles of democracy and freedom, the immediate response of nations must be to band together to condemn and combat terrorist groups and to ostracize countries that support terrorism. The coming struggle is not a war between religions, but one between democracy and tyranny.

Thank you, President of the General Assembly Dr. Han Seung-Soo. Thank you, Secretary General Kofi Annan.

Thank you very much for the opportunity to speak, and for the consideration you've shown the City in putting off your General Session. As I explained to the Secretary General and the President of the General Assembly, our City is now open, and any time we can arrange it, we look forward to having your heads of state and your foreign ministers here for that session.

A vicious attack

On September 11th, 2001, New York City—the most diverse City in the world—was viciously attacked in an unprovoked act of war. More than five thousand innocent men, women, and children of every race, religion, and ethnicity are lost. Among these were people from 80 different nations. To their representatives here today, I offer my condolences to you

From Rudolph W. Giuliani's "Opening Remarks to the United Nations General Assembly Special Session on Terrorism," October 1, 2001.

as well on behalf of all New Yorkers who share this loss with you. This was the deadliest terrorist attack in history. It claimed more lives than Pearl Harbor or D-Day.

This was not just an attack on the City of New York or on the United States of America. It was an attack on the very idea of a free, inclusive, and civil society.

It was a direct assault on the founding principles of the United Nations itself. The Preamble to the UN Charter states that this organization exists "to reaffirm faith in fundamental human rights, in the dignity and worth of the human person . . . to practice tolerance and live together in peace as good neighbors . . . [and] to unite our strength to maintain international peace and security."

Indeed, this vicious attack places in jeopardy the whole purpose of the United Nations.

This massive attack was intended to break our spirit. It has not done that.

Terrorism is based on the persistent and deliberate violation of fundamental human rights. With bullets and bombs—and now with hijacked airplanes—terrorists deny the dignity of human life. Terrorism preys particularly on cultures and communities that practice openness and tolerance. Their targeting of innocent civilians mocks the efforts of those who seek to live together in peace as neighbors. It defies the very notion of being a neighbor.

This massive attack was intended to break our spirit. It has not done that. It has made us stronger, more determined and more resolved.

The bravery of our firefighters, our police officers, our emergency workers, and civilians we may never learn of, in saving over 25,000 lives that day—carrying out the most effective rescue operation in our history—inspires all of us. I am very honored to have with me, as their representative, the Fire Commissioner of New York City, Tom Von Essen, and the Police Commissioner of New York City, Bernard Kerik.

The determination, resolve, and leadership of President George W. Bush has unified America and all decent men and women around the world.

The response of many of your nations—your leaders and people—spontaneously demonstrating in the days after the attack your support for New York and America, and your understanding of what needs to be done to remove the threat of terrorism, gives us great, great hope that we will prevail.

America's response and beliefs

The strength of America's response, please understand, flows from the principles upon which we stand.

Americans are not a single ethnic group.

Americans are not of one race or one religion.

Americans emerge from all your nations.

We are defined as Americans by our beliefs—not by our ethnic origins, our race or our religion. Our beliefs in religious freedom, political freedom, and economic freedom—that's what makes an American. Our belief in democracy, the rule of law, and respect for human life—that's how you become an American. It is these very principles—and the opportunities these principles give to so many to create a better life for themselves and their families—that make America, and New York, a "shining city on a hill."

There is no nation, and no City, in the history of the world that has seen more immigrants, in less time, than America. People continue to come here in large numbers to seek freedom, opportunity, decency, and civility.

Each of your nations—I am certain—has contributed citizens to the United States and to New York. I believe I can take every one of you someplace in New York City, where you can find someone from your country, someone from your village or town, that speaks your language and practices your religion. In each of your lands there are many who are Americans in spirit, by virtue of their commitment to our shared principles.

It is tragic and perverse that it is because of these very principles—particularly our religious, political and economic freedoms—that we find ourselves under attack by terrorists.

Our freedom threatens them, because they know that if our ideas of freedom gain a foothold among their people it will destroy their power. So they strike out against us to keep those ideas from reaching their people.

The terrorists are wrong, and in fact evil, in their mass destruction of human life in the name of addressing alleged injustices.

The best long-term deterrent to terrorism—obviously—is the spread of our principles of freedom, democracy, the rule of law, and respect for human life. The more that spreads around the globe, the safer we will all be. These are very powerful ideas and once they gain a foothold, they cannot be stopped.

In fact, the rise that we have seen in terrorism and terrorist groups, I believe, is in no small measure a response to the spread of these ideas of freedom and democracy to many nations, particularly over the past 15 years.

The terrorists have no ideas or ideals with which to combat freedom and democracy. So their only defense is to strike out against innocent civilians, destroying human life in massive numbers and hoping to deter all of us from our pursuit and expansion of freedom.

Acting together to stop terrorists

But the long-term deterrent of spreading our ideals throughout the world is just not enough, and may never be realized, if we do not act—and act together—to remove the clear and present danger posed by terrorism and terrorists.

The United Nations must hold accountable any country that supports or condones terrorism, otherwise you will fail in your primary mission as peacekeeper.

It must ostracize any nation that supports terrorism.

It must isolate any nation that remains neutral in the fight against terrorism.

Now is the time, in the words of the UN Charter, "to unite our strength to maintain international peace and security." This is not a time for further study or vague directives. The evidence of terrorism's brutality and inhumanity—of its contempt for life and the concept of peace—is lying beneath the rubble of the World Trade Center less than two miles from where we meet today.

No room for neutrality

Look at that destruction, that massive, senseless, cruel loss of human life . . . and then I ask you to look in your hearts and recognize that there is no room for neutrality on the issue of terrorism. You're either with civilization or with terrorists.

On one side is democracy, the rule of law, and respect for human life; on the other is tyranny, arbitrary executions, and mass murder.

We're right and they're wrong. It's as simple as that.

And by that I mean that America and its allies are right about democracy, about religious, political, and economic freedom.

The terrorists are wrong, and in fact evil, in their mass destruction of human life in the name of addressing alleged injustices.

No excuses for terrorism

Let those who say that we must understand the reasons for terrorism come with me to the thousands of funerals we are having in New York City and explain those insane, maniacal reasons to the children who will grow up without fathers and mothers, to the parents who have had their children ripped from them for no reason at all.

Instead, I ask each of you to allow me to say at those funerals that your nation stands with America in making a solemn promise and pledge that we will achieve unconditional victory over terrorism and terrorists.

There is no excuse for mass murder, just as there is no excuse for genocide. Those who practice terrorism—murdering or victimizing innocent civilians—lose any right to have their cause understood by decent people and lawful nations.

On this issue—terrorism—the United Nations must draw a line. The era of moral relativism between those who practice or condone terrorism, and those nations who stand up against it, must end. Moral relativism does not have a place in this discussion and debate.

There is no moral way to sympathize with grossly immoral actions. And by trying to do that, unfortunately, a fertile field has been created in which terrorism has grown.

Ways to fight terrorists

The best and most practical way to promote peace is to stand up to terror and intimidation. The Security Council's unanimous passage of Resolution 1373, adopting wide ranging anti-terrorism measures in the international community is a very good first step. It's necessary to establish accountability for the subsidizing of terrorism.

As a former United States Attorney, I am particularly encouraged that the UN has answered President Bush's call to cut terrorists off from their money and their funding. It's enormously important. We've done that successfully with organized crime groups in America. By taking away their ability to mass large amounts of money, you take away their ability to have others carry on their functioning for them, even if they are removed, arrested, prosecuted, or eliminated through war or through law enforcement. It cuts off the life-blood of the organization. So I believe this is a very good first step.

But now it's up to the member states to enforce this and other aspects of the resolution, and for the United Nations to enforce these new mechanisms to take the financial base away from the terrorists. Take away their money, take away their access to money, and you reduce their ability to carry out complex missions.

Each of you is sitting in this room because of your country's commitment to being part of the family of nations. We need to unite as a family as never before—across all our differences, in recognition of the fact that the United Nations stands for the proposition that as human beings we have more in common than divides us.

If you need to be reminded of this, you don't need to look very far. Just go outside for a walk in the streets and parks of New York City. You can't walk a block in New York City without seeing somebody that looks different than you, acts different than you, talks different than you, believes different than you. If you grow up in New York City, you learn that. And if you're an intelligent or decent person, you learn that all those differences are nothing in comparison to the things that unite us.

This is not a dispute between religions or ethnic groups.

We are a City of immigrants—unlike any other City—within a nation of immigrants. Like the victims of the World Trade Center attack, we are of every race, religion, and ethnicity. Our diversity has always been our greatest source of strength. It's the thing that renews us and revives us in every generation—our openness to new people from all over the world.

So from the first day of this attack, an attack on New York and America, and I believe an attack on the basic principles that underlie this organization, I have told the people of New York that we should not allow this to divide us, because then we would really lose what this City is all about. We have very strong and vibrant Arab and Muslim communities in New York City. They are an equally important part of the life of our City. We respect their religious beliefs. We respect everybody's religious beliefs—that's what America's about, that's what New York City is about. I have urged New Yorkers not to engage in any form of group blame or group hatred. This is exactly the evil that we are confronting with these terrorists. And if we are going to prevail over terror, our ideals, principles, and values must transcend all forms of prejudice.

This is a very important part of the struggle against terrorism.

This is not a dispute between religions or ethnic groups. All religions, all decent people, are united in their desire to achieve peace, and understand that we have to eliminate terrorism. We're not divided about this.

There have been many days in New York when I was running for Mayor, and then since I've been Mayor, when I would have a weekend in which I would go to a mosque on Friday, and a synagogue on Saturday, and a church—sometimes two churches—on a Sunday. And by the time I finished, I would say to myself, 'I know that we're getting through to God.' We're talking to him in every language that He understands, we're using every liturgy that exists, and I know that we are getting through to the same God, even though we may be doing it in slightly different ways. God is known by many different names and many different traditions, but identified by one consistent feeling, love. Love for humanity, particularly love for our children. Love does eventually conquer hate, but it needs our help. Good intentions alone are not enough to conquer evil.

> *The only acceptable result is the complete and total eradication of terrorism.*

Remember British Prime Minister Neville Chamberlain, who—armed only with good intentions—negotiated with the Nazis and emerged hopeful that he had achieved peace in his time. Hitler's wave of terror was only encouraged by these attempts at appeasement. At the cost of millions of lives, we learned that words—though important—are not enough to guarantee peace. It is action alone that counts.

For the UN, and individual nations, decisive action is needed to stop terrorism from ever orphaning another child.

The resilience of life

That's for nations. For individuals, the most effective course of action they can take to aid our recovery is to be determined to go ahead with their lives. We can't let terrorists change the way we live—otherwise they will have succeeded.

In some ways, the resilience of life in New York City is the ultimate sign of defiance to terrorism. We call ourselves the Capital of the World in large part because we are the most diverse City in the world, home to the United Nations. The spirit of unity amid all our diversity has never been stronger.

On Saturday night [September 29, 2001] I walked through Times Square, it was crowded, it was bright, it was lively. Thousands of people were visiting from all parts of the United States and all parts of the world. And many of them came up to me and shook my hand and patted me on the back and said, "We're here because we want to show our support for the City of New York." And that's why there has never been a better time to come to New York City.

I say to people across the country and around the world: if you were planning to come to New York sometime in the future, come here now.

Come to enjoy our thousands of restaurants, museums, theaters, sporting events, and shopping . . . but also come to take a stand against terrorism.

We need to heed the words of a hymn that I, and the Police Commissioner, and the Fire Commissioner, have heard at the many funerals and memorial services that we've gone to in the last two weeks. The hymn begins, "Be Not Afraid."

Freedom from Fear is a basic human right. We need to reassert our right to live free from fear with greater confidence and determination than ever before . . . here in New York City . . . across America . . . and around the World. With one clear voice, unanimously, we need to say that we will not give in to terrorism.

Surrounded by our friends of every faith, we know that this is not a clash of civilizations; it is a conflict between murderers and humanity.

This is not a question of retaliation or revenge. It is a matter of justice leading to peace. The only acceptable result is the complete and total eradication of terrorism.

New Yorkers are strong and resilient. We are unified. And we will not yield to terror. We do not let fear make our decisions for us.

We choose to live in freedom.

Thank you, and God bless you.

19

The Attacks Revealed the Importance of the Public Sector

Jeff Faux

Jeff Faux is president of the Economic Policy Institute, a nonprofit think tank that performs research and analyses on issues affecting low- and middle-income workers.

Prior to September 11, 2001, it was fashionable in many circles to denigrate the public sector and public service. Such attitudes changed when terrorists attacked the World Trade Center and the Pentagon. Americans turned to firefighters and other public workers and institutions for help following the attacks. In addition, the attacks revealed the price America has paid for making airport security a privatized matter in which low costs and wages were more important than reliable security.

There is no silver lining to the cloud of horror that descended on America on September 11, 2001. And the avalanche of pain, terror, and death we have witnessed may be just the beginning.

But life, as always, slowly picks up and moves on. Despite the nagging sense that it is unseemly to begin thinking about the economic consequences, the country is once again back in the market. Investors are selling the stocks of insurance companies and airlines, buying those of military contractors and companies that will benefit from the new security-conscious society. Economists are calculating the gains and losses and guessing about the odds of a recession.

Many are engaged in burying the dead and tending to the survivors, or facing the awesome responsibility of satisfying the national demand for action that serves justice rather than multiplying evil. Those of us who are going back to business have an obligation, as we do, to reflect on what we have seen.

The attacks of September 11 revealed some truths about the American political economy that have been obscured in recent years.

The working class

One is just how much of our economy is made up of what used to be called the "working class"—the non-supervisory, non-college-educated people who make up 70 percent of our labor force. For the last half-dozen years the media saw economic trends through the eyes of the glamorous, globe-trotting, business executive—to the point where it seemed to many that they must represent the vast majority of American workers. And one could hardly find a more fitting symbol of the new global economy than the World Trade Center—surrounded in the evening with a herd of sleek limousines waiting to serve the masters of the universe at the end of the day.

And yet, it turns out that the building was run by thousands of data clerks and secretaries, waiters and dishwashers, janitors and telecommunication repair people. The roll of trade unions mourning their dead is long: firefighters, hotel and restaurant employees, police, communication workers, service employees, teachers, federal employees, pilots and flight attendants, longshoremen, professional engineers, operating engineers, the electrical workers, federal employees, building trades, and state, county, and municipal employees.

And many were in no union, meaning job insecurity, no benefits, and certainly no limousines.

The importance of government

A second insight revealed by the awful gaping hole in the Manhattan skyline was how ill-served we have been by a politics that perpetuates the illusion that we are all on our own and, in particular, holds the institutions of public service in contempt. For two decades, politicians of both parties have celebrated the pursuit of private gain over public service. Shrinking government has become a preoccupation of political leaders through deregulation, privatization, and cuts in public services.

> *The attacks . . . revealed some truths about the American political economy that have been obscured in recent years.*

One result is that the U.S. is the only major nation that leaves airline and airport security in the hands of private corporations, which by their very nature are motivated to spend as little as possible. So the system was tossed in the lap of lowest-bid contractors who hired people for minimum wages. Training has been inadequate and supervision extremely lax. Turnover was 126 percent a year and the average employee stayed in airline security for only six months. Getting a job at Burger King or McDonald's represented upward mobility for the average security worker. In an anti-government political climate the airline corporations were able to shrug off the government inspections that consistently revealed how easy it was to bring weapons on board. The competition for customers sacrificed safety to avoid any inconvenience. How else to explain the insane notion that a 3-1/2 inch knife blade is not a weapon?

Private provision of public services has been the dominant philosophy of government in our time. Only natural, the economists told us. People were motivated by money. It's human nature. "Greed is good," said the movie character in the send-up of Wall Street—a sentiment echoed by politicians of both parties. "Collective solutions are a thing of the past. . . . The era of big government is over. . . . You are on your own." Public service was "old" economy, just for losers. A teacher in New York City schools starts at $30,000. A brand new securities lawyer starts at $120,000. Does anyone believe that this represents sensible priorities?

When the chips are down, where do we turn? To the government's firefighters, police officers, rescue teams.

And does anyone believe that the firefighters who marched into that inferno did it for money? Does anyone think that people working for a private company hiring people for as little as possible would have had the same motivation—would have been as efficient? At the moment when efficiency really counts?

When the chips are down, where do we turn? To the government's firefighters, police officers, rescue teams. To the nonprofit sectors' blood banks and shelters. And to Big Government's army, navy, and air force. During his campaign, the president of the United States constantly complained that the people knew how to spend their money better than the government did. Overnight, we just appropriated $40 billion for the government to spend however it sees fit. Who else would we trust?

The stock market itself made one point. Despite calls for investors to exercise patriotic restraint, the market opened with an avalanche of sell orders, driving the Dow to its largest point loss in history. As one broker said, "This is how capitalism is supposed to work." Just so. The market is about prices, not values.

America's identity

Finally, perhaps we learned something about our national identity.

It is common—almost a cliché—among political philosophers and pundits to define America as an "exception." For many, America's exceptionalism means that it is the best place to get rich. For others, it is our unique set of laws—our Bill of Rights. Still others see America not in national terms at all, but as a patchwork of ethnic groups and regional interests.

There is some truth in all of these views. But those who risked and gave their lives—both the public servants and the brave civilian passengers who rushed the terrorists and forced the airliner down in Pennsylvania before it could get to Washington—are unlikely to have acted out of reverence for the deregulated market or for our court system or for some ethnic or religious loyalty.

Everything we know tells us that they acted as human beings responding to the agony of other human beings, or trying in one last desperate effort to spare their country more damage, not because it is the world's superpower but simply because it is their country. No country has a monopoly on simple patriotism.

If America is, as the politicians often remind us, the "last best hope" for humankind, then it is not because we as individuals are exceptional and different from the rest of the world, but because we are much the same—full of the normal set of human traits, which at times of stress often bring out the best in us.

It is obvious that we can no longer rely on our exceptionalism to keep us safe. In the coming weeks and months and years we are likely to be reminded of that. To get through this, we need to be disabused quickly of the illusion that we are all on our own. America's strength, like the strength of any other society, is in our ability to be there for each other.

20

The Attacks Marked the End of the Post–Cold War Era

Robert D. Kaplan

Robert D. Kaplan is a senior fellow at the New American Foundation
and the author of seven books on international affairs, including The
Coming Anarchy: Shattering the Dreams of the Post–Cold War.

The September 2001 terrorist attacks marked the end of an era
that began in 1989 with the fall of the Berlin Wall and the end of
the cold war, during which the United States tried to impose its vision of democracy on the world. The American people learned in
the 2001 attacks that preservation of security at home and power
abroad is the primary function of foreign policy. They will tolerate alliances with questionable regimes and restrictions on their
own liberties in the coming struggle against terrorism.

President George W. Bush saw the big change needed in America's foreign policy long before the intellectuals and the media did. Bush's campaign rhetoric and subsequent foreign affairs strategy—in which he has
sought to clear the decks of nonessential overseas involvements in order
to concentrate on security threats for a new military and technological
age—while wrong in some specifics, have been proven tragically prescient
in their overall conception. It is not that Bush foresaw specifically the recent terrorist attack; but his insistence that humanitarian missions are not
a signal priority in a dangerous world—where America has to look after its
own—showed considerable instinct regarding what has happened.

Moreover, his conception is firmly grounded in history. It realizes
that America's continued dominance—like that of Britain and Rome before it—is not certain. Thus, improving the chances of America remain-
ing a dominant power requires the husbanding of our foreign policy resources and the continued adaptation of our military establishment to
new kinds of threats. What seems absolutely ahistorical today is the vision of a permanently secure America that will have the luxury of open-
ended overseas deployments in places such as Bosnia and Kosovo.

The latest spasm of triumphalist idealism—first injected into our con-

From "U.S. Foreign Policy, Brought Back Home," by Robert D. Kaplan, *The Washington Post*,
September 23, 2001. Copyright © 2001 by The Washington Post Company. Reprinted by
permission of the author.

duct of foreign affairs by President Woodrow Wilson in the early 20th century—ended with the destruction of the World Trade Center. We can no longer afford the luxury of noblesse oblige in foreign policy now that the assumption of security at home is absent. Foreign policy must return to what it traditionally has been: the diplomatic aspect of national security rather than a branch of Holocaust studies.

End of an era

The 20th century did not, as many have claimed, end ahead of schedule in November 1989, with the fall of the Berlin Wall. The 1990s were not the beginning of a new, more enlightened era in international relations; rather, they were a coda to the Cold War in Eastern Europe and a period when the World War II Nazi slaughter of the Jews was uppermost in our minds as we tried to grapple with ethnic hatreds in the Balkans and elsewhere.

The 20th century ended behind schedule—in September 2001. The post–Cold War era will be seen in future decades as a 12-year interregnum— from the collapse of the Berlin Wall to the collapse of the World Trade Center—in which the United States, basking in its victory over communism and with a seemingly unstoppable economy, tried to impose its moral vision on the rest of the world, while neglecting its homeland defense. Security became lax at airports, and the military and intelligence establishments were neither reformed nor beefed up, even as we dispatched troops to trouble spots only marginally related to our national interests. But following the most deadly terrorist incident in history, the American people have learned that to influence the world morally requires first the preservation of their own security, as well as their reputation for power.

The need for security

The need to maintain power and security must now come first: Our values will follow in their wake. After all, democratization in places such as Eastern Europe has not been a natural and inevitable event; it is a direct consequence of our Cold War military victory. If the destruction of the World Trade Center diminishes America's reputation for power—if it seems to paralyze this nation and make it appear unduly fearful—the democratic values that we promote abroad will be similarly eclipsed.

Now we are truly in an age of new technological threats—particularly chemical and biological weapons—that will return us to an earlier epoch, at the beginning of the 19th century, when realism flourished under men like John Adams and Alexander Hamilton while we were being threatened on our own continent by the French and Spanish, as well as by the British fleet. Such realism posits that foreign affairs entails a separate, sadder morality than the kind we apply in domestic policy and in our daily lives. That is because domestically we operate under the rule of law, while the wider world is an anarchic realm where we are forced to take the law into our own hands. This is a distinction that the public will tolerate now that its security has been shaken. The public will likely have little trouble comprehending why Bush may have to perpetrate a certain amount of evil in coming months and even years in order to do a greater amount of good.

Even our vision of democracy must now undergo subtle realistic alteration. Rather than demand that countries such as Pakistan, Egypt and Tunisia democratize, we will have to increasingly tolerate benign dictatorships and various styles of hybrid regimes, provided that they help us in our new struggle. Nor will there be anything amoral or cynical about that. For, in the long term, the world will be a better place if the American people feel secure.

In the new age of warfare, speed will be the killer variable, making democratic consultation an afterthought. Striking terrorist cells before they strike us—hitting not just hijackers, but the computer command centers of our future adversaries before they can launch computer viruses on the United States, for instance—will need to be accomplished by surprise if it is to be effective. That will leave no time for the president to sound out the public or even many members of Congress.

Liberal elites vs. the American public

The public will not likely mind, provided the attacks are seen to contribute to its safety. The more prosperous a society is, the more moral compromises it will be ready to make to preserve its material well-being. One of the false beliefs of the age of globalization has been that economic power has superseded military power. In fact, the reality is the reverse. The greater the economic power, the more military power is required to protect it, especially because of the envy and resentment that such economic power generates. Blather about how financial markets are the new foundation of power—the mantra of optimists transfixed by globalization throughout the 1990s—can only be indulged in when the physical security of those markets can be taken for granted. And it no longer can be.

Unfettered idealism of the sort associated with Woodrow Wilson is feasible only so long as the United States feels itself geographically invulnerable. Whenever we have failed to implement our lofty vision abroad, we have been able to retreat back across great oceans, as we did after World War I. Today, however, because of technology, places such as the Middle East are as close to us as the Ottoman Turkish Empire was to Europe. Oceanic distance from global hot spots such as the West Bank no longer exists. The duo of idealism and isolationism will have to be replaced by realism and constant engagement: engagement consistent with our national interest.

The 20th century ended behind schedule—in September 2001.

In his novel "The Secret Agent," Joseph Conrad wrote that the greatest threat to terrorism is ordinary citizens: the throngs of working- and middle-class people who—because they just want to get on with their lives—are willing to trust the grim details of their protection to the police and other security organs. Following Sept. 11, 2001, these ordinary citizens will determine foreign policy. It has ceased to be the realm of cosmopolitan elites in the media and academia, who for the past 12 years have been more concerned with universal values of justice than with our national security. But the elites' dream of an international civilization has been stillborn. Globalization, like the Industrial Revolution before it, is merely a phase of technological development—not a system of international security. Wars will go on, because beyond the liberal elites, humanity is as divided as ever.

Organizations to Contact

The editors have compiled the following list of organizations concerned with the issues debated in this book. The descriptions are derived from materials provided by the organizations. All have publications or information available for interested readers. The list was compiled on the date of publication of the present volume; the information provided here may change. Be aware that many organizations take several weeks or longer to respond to inquiries, so allow as much time as possible.

American Civil Liberties Union (ACLU)
125 Broad St., 18th Floor, New York, NY 10004-2400
(212) 549-2500
e-mail: aclu@aclu.org • website: www.aclu.org

The American Civil Liberties Union is a national organization that works to defend Americans' civil rights guaranteed by the U.S. Constitution, arguing that measures to protect national security should not compromise fundamental civil liberties. It publishes and distributes policy statements, pamphlets, and press releases with titles such as "In Defense of Freedom in a Time of Crisis" and "National ID Cards: 5 Reasons Why They Should Be Rejected."

American Enterprise Institute (AEI)
1150 17th St. NW, Washington, DC 20036
(202) 862-5800 • fax: (202) 862-7177
website: www.aei.org

The American Enterprise Institute for Public Policy Research is a scholarly research institute that is dedicated to preserving limited government, private enterprise, and a strong foreign policy and national defense. It publishes books including *Study of Revenge: The First World Trade Center Attack* and *Saddam Hussein's War Against America*. Articles about terrorism and September 11 can be found in its magazine, *American Enterprise*, and on its website.

Anti-Defamation League (ADL)
823 United Nations Plaza, New York, NY 10017
(212) 885-7700 • fax: (212) 867-0779
website: www.adl.org

The Anti-Defamation League is a human relations organization dedicated to combating all forms of prejudice and bigotry. The league has placed a spotlight on terrorism and on the dangers posed for extremism. Its website records reactions to the September 11, 2001, terrorist incidents by both extremist and mainstream organizations, provides background information on Osama bin Laden, and furnishes other materials on terrorism and the Middle East. The ADL also maintains a bimonthly online newsletter, *Frontline*.

The Brookings Institution
1775 Massachusetts Ave. NW, Washington, DC 20036
(202) 797-6000 • fax: (202) 797-6004
e-mail: brookinfo@brook.edu • website: www.brookings.org

The institution, founded in 1927, is a think tank that conducts research and education in foreign policy, economics, government, and the social sciences. In 2001 it began America's Response to Terrorism, a project that provides briefings and analysis to the public and which is featured on the center's website. Other publications include the quarterly *Brookings Review*, periodic *Policy Briefs*, and books including *Terrorism and U.S. Foreign Policy*.

CATO Institute
1000 Massachusetts Ave. NW, Washington, DC 20001-5403
(202) 842-0200 • fax: (202) 842-3490
e-mail: cato@cato.org • website: www.cato.org

The Institute is a nonpartisan public policy research foundation dedicated to limiting the role of government and protecting individual liberties. It publishes the quarterly magazine *Regulation*, the bimonthly *Cato Policy Report*, and numerous policy papers and articles. Works on terrorism include "Does U.S. Intervention Overseas Breed Terrorism?" and "Military Tribunals No Answer."

Center for Strategic and International Studies (CSIS)
1800 K St. NW, Suite 400, Washington, DC 20006
(202) 887-0200 • fax: (202) 775-3199
website: www.csis.org

The center works to provide world leaders with strategic insights and policy options on current and emerging global issues. It publishes books including *To Prevail: An American Strategy for the Campaign Against Terrorism*, the *Washington Quarterly*, a journal on political, economic, and security issues, and other publications including reports that can be downloaded from its website.

Council on American-Islamic Relations (CAIR)
453 New Jersey Ave. SE, Washington, DC 20003
(202) 488-8787 • fax: (202) 488-0833
e-mail: cair@cair-net.org • website: www.cair-net.org

CAIR is a nonprofit membership organization that presents an Islamic perspective on public policy issues and challenges the misrepresentation of Islam and Muslims. It publishes the quarterly newsletter *Faith in Action* and other various publications on Muslims in the United States. Its website includes statements condemning both the September 11 attacks and discrimination against Muslims.

Federal Aviation Administration (FAA)
800 Independence Ave. SW, Washington, DC 20591
(800) 322-7873 • fax: (202) 267-3484
website: www.faa.gov

The Federal Aviation Administration is the component of the U.S. Department of Transportation whose primary responsibility is the safety of civil aviation. The FAA's major functions include regulating civil aviation to promote safety and fulfill the requirements of national defense. Among its publications are *Technology Against Terrorism, Air Piracy, Airport Security, and International Terrorism: Winning the War Against Hijackers*, and *Security Tips for Air Travelers*.

Institute for Policy Studies (IPS)
733 15th St. NW, Suite 1020, Washington, DC 20005
(202) 234-9382 • fax (202) 387-7915
website: www.ips-dc.org

The Institute for Policy Studies is a progressive think tank that works to develop societies built around the values of justice and nonviolence. It publishes reports including *Global Perspectives: A Media Guide to Foreign Policy Experts*. Numerous articles and interviews on September 11 and terrorism are available on its website.

International Policy Institute of Counter-Terrorism (ICT)
PO Box 167, Herzlia 46150, Israel
972-9-9527277 • fax: 972-9-9513073
e-mail: mail@ict.org.il • website: www.ict.org.il

ICT is a research institute dedicated to developing public policy solutions to international terrorism. The ICT website is a comprehensive resource on terrorism and counterterrorism, featuring an extensive database on terrorist attacks and organizations, including al-Qaida.

Islamic Supreme Council of America (ISCA)
1400 16th St. NW, Room B112, Washington, DC 20036
(202) 939-3400 • fax: (202) 939-3410
e-mail: staff@islamicsupremecouncil.org
website: www.islamicsupremecouncil.org

The ISCA is a nongovernmental religious organization that promotes Islam in America both by providing practical solutions to American Muslims in integrating Islamic teachings with American culture and by teaching non-Muslims that Islam is a religion of moderation, peace, and tolerance. It strongly condemns Islamic extremists and all forms of terrorism. Its website includes statements, commentaries, and reports on terrorism, including *Usama bin Laden: A Legend Gone Wrong* and *Jihad: A Misunderstood Concept from Islam*.

Middle East Media Research Institute (MEMRI)
PO Box 27837, Washington, DC 20038-7837
(202) 955-9070 • fax: (202) 955-9077
e-mail: memri@erols.com • website: www.memri.org

MEMRI translates and disseminates articles and commentaries from Middle East media sources and provides original research and analysis on the region. Its Jihad and Terrorism Studies Project monitors radical Islamist groups and individuals and their reactions to acts of terrorism around the world.

U.S. Department of State, Counterterrorism Office
Office of Public Affairs, Room 2507
U.S. Department of State
2201 C St. NW, Washington, DC 20520
(202) 647-4000
e-mail: secretary@state.gov • website: www.state.gov/s/ct

The office works to develop and implement American counterterrorism strategy and to improve cooperation with foreign governments. Articles and speeches by government officials are available at its website.

War Resisters League (WRL)
339 Lafayette St., New York, NY 10012
(212) 228-0450 • fax: (212) 228-6193
e-mail: wrl@warresisters.org • website: www.warresisters.org

The WRL, founded in 1923, believes that all war is a crime against humanity, and advocates nonviolent methods to create a just and democratic society. It publishes the magazine *The Nonviolent Activist*. Articles from that magazine, as well as other commentary and resources about September 11 and America's war against terrorism, are available on its website.

Bibliography

Books

Yonah Alexander and Michael S. Swetman	*Usama bin Laden's al-Qaida: Profile of a Terrorist Network*. Ardsley, NY: Transnational Publishers, 2001.
Peter L. Bergen	*Holy War Inc.: Inside the Secret World of Osama bin Laden*. New York: Free Press, 2001.
Noam Chomsky	*9-11*. New York: Seven Stories Press, 2001.
Martha Crenshaw and John Pimlott, eds.	*Encyclopedia of World Terrorism*. Armonk, NY: Sharpe Reference, 1997.
Laura K. Egendorf, ed.	*Terrorism: Opposing Viewpoints*. San Diego: Greenhaven Press, 2000.
Philip B. Heymann	*Terrorism and America: A Commonsense Strategy for a Democratic Society*. Cambridge, MA: MIT Press, 1998.
James F. Hoge Jr. and Gideon Rose, eds.	*How Did This Happen? Terrorism and the New War*. New York: Public Affairs, 2001.
Jessica Kornbluth and Jessica Papin, eds.	*Because We Are Americans: What We Discovered on September 11, 2001*. New York: Warner Books, 2001.
Bernard Lewis	*What Went Wrong? Western Impact and Middle Eastern Response*. New York: Oxford University Press, 2001.
Jon Ronson	*Adventures with Extremists*. New York: Simon and Schuster, 2002.
Barbara Shangle, ed.	*Day of Terror, September 11, 2001*. Beaverton, OR: American Products, 2001.
Strobe Talbott and Nayan Chanda, eds.	*The Age of Terror: America and the World After September 11*. New York: Basic Books, 2002.

Periodicals

David Aaron	"The New Twilight Struggle," *American Prospect*, October 22, 2001.
Michael Albert and Stephen R. Shalom	"September 11 and Its Aftermath," *Z Magazine*, October 2001.
Jonathan Alter	"Blame America at Your Peril," *Newsweek*, October 15, 2001.
Benjamin R. Barber	"Beyond Jihad vs. McWorld," *Nation*, January 21, 2002.

86

Max Boot — "The Case for American Empire," *Weekly Standard*, October 15, 2001.

Business Week — "Keeping America's Gates Open. Just Watch Them Better," November 19, 2001.

David Carr — "The Futility of Homeland Defense," *Atlantic Monthly*, January 2002.

Congressional Digest — "War on Terrorism," November 2001.

Economist — "The Day the World Changed," September 13, 2001.

Richard Falk — "Defining a Just War," *Nation*, October 29, 2001.

John Lewis Gaddis — "Setting Right a Dangerous World," *Chronicle of Higher Education,* January 11, 2002.

Adolfo Gilly — "The Faceless Enemy," *NACLA Report on the Americas*, November/December 2001.

Lee Griffith — "Terror and the Hope Within," *The Other Side*, January/February 2002.

Michael Howard — "What's in a Name?: How to Fight Terrorism," *Foreign Affairs*, January/February 2002.

David E. Kaplan and Kevin Whitelaw — "The CEO of Terror, Inc." *U.S. News & World Report*, October 1, 2001.

James Kitfield — "Ending State Terror," *National Journal,* October 2, 2001.

Charles Krauthammer — "The Real New World Order," *Weekly Standard*, November 12, 2001.

Lewis H. Lapham — "Drums Along the Potomac," *Harper's Magazine*, November 2001.

Michael Lerner — "The Case for Peace," *Time*, October 1, 2001.

Brink Lindsey — "Poor Choice—Why Globalization Didn't Create 9/11," *New Republic*, November 12, 2001.

Richard Lowry — "Profiles in Cowardice," *National Review*, January 28, 2002.

Wayne Madsen — "Why Wasn't Bush Warned?" *In These Times*, October 15, 2001.

W.J.T. Mitchell — "911: Criticism and Crisis," *Critical Inquiry*, Winter 2002.

Chris Mooney — "Holy War," *American Prospect*, December 17, 2001.

Sabeel Rahman — "Another New World Order? Multilateralism in the Aftermath of September 11," *Harvard International Review*, Winter 2002.

Richard Rhodes et al.   "What Terror Keeps Teaching Us," *New York Times Magazine*, September 23, 2001.

Matthew Rothschild   "The New McCarthyism," *Progressive*, January 2002.

Arundhati Roy   "New World Disorder," *In These Times*, November 26, 2001.

Nelson D. Schwartz   "Learning from Israel," *Fortune*, January 21, 2002.

Benjamin Schwartz and Christopher Layne   "A New Grand Strategy," *Atlantic Monthly*, January 2002.

Jay Tolson   "Early Drafts of History," *U.S. News & World Report*, January 14, 2002.

Index